...THEN WHY DO I HAVE TOENAILS?

How to be the best Atheist you can be.

The unedited version.

by
Thom Phelps

www.toenailsbook.com

ISBN 1434830241

All artwork in this book is original art by the author, protected by copyright, with the exception of the "I dreamed I was God" illustration which is a legally purchased royalty-free image, graphically manipulated from the original for use in this book.

Cover design and original artwork by the author.

Cover photo by Betta Phelps.

Pedicure by Shalom Spa, Chandler, AZ.

The short stories in this book are works of fiction. All characters, events, and dialogue are drawn from the author's imagination and are not to be construed as actual. Any resemblance to real events or persons, living or dead, is entirely coincidental.

*For Danny, whose slip into religious fanatacism
inspired me to write these thoughts.*

Contents

So you think you're an Atheist

Introduction

Welcome to your new God-free life. This handbook will not only gently guide you down the path toward Atheism, it will also teach you how to be the best Atheist you can be. You've taken the first step. All you need to do now is read a few pages, say the magic words revealed to you subliminally through the text, then sit back and relax as all connections to any religion or deity are severed forever. The shackles will fall away and the rest of your life will be filled with guilt-free happiness.

Don't worry. That's not how it works.

This book is my explanation, in simple layman's terms, why I choose to be an Atheist. I'm writing it for a friend who doesn't understand why I don't believe in God after he proved God's existence to me. (He prayed that a dog he poisoned wouldn't die, and miraculously it didn't. *Hallelujah, God be praised!*) So, at one end of the universe a dog gets poisoned, and at the other end of the universe you find yourself reading this book. Kind of creepy. I'll go into details in Chapter 3.

I also intend for this book to be used to help other Atheists explain why they don't believe. I hope people who have heard of Atheists but don't know what it means to be one will read it for some insight into our world. It is for new Atheists who want to learn how to be **good at being an Atheist without all the anger and hatred toward** religion and believers that so often goes along with disbelief. And it's for bad Atheists who want to learn to be good people despite there being no eternal punishment for doing bad things. All of these reasons are what I mean in the sub-title when I say, "How to be the best Atheist you can be."

For those Atheists who plan on giving this book to your Christian roommate and expect him or her to become an Atheist tomorrow, don't. If anything, it will probably reinforce their resolve.

How is it put together?

Originally I wrote this as an epistle, a letter from me to the friend I mentioned above. Then I read a book about self publishing that said, "if you really want to make money in this arena, you need to write a self-help book." So I took that advice and decided to make half of this a letter about my personal experience with Atheism and half of it a how-to book on becoming an Atheist. That way on-line book stores could easily classify it under three categories: self-help, how-to and religion. Hopefully some will also categorize it under comedy and humorous stories that piss off religious fanatics.

Each chapter begins with a little piece of self-help for the reader, followed by my thoughts on religion, religious people, Atheism, etc. There is no profound message hidden between the lines. Since it's my pulpit, I will occasionally rail against religious hypocrites, intolerant fundamentalists, and some of the more kooky religions I've seen. And don't worry about me quoting the great philosophers or using big words like existensialism, transmutation, or ecumenical. If you want to read a book on philosophy, go buy one. Plenty have already been written.

It's intentionally written at an 8th grade level for four reasons:

1. I'm not very smart.

2. I'm writing it for someone who grew up with severe dyslexia, has a short vocabulary, and has a hard time reading long sentences.

3. Most fundamentalists I know who believe in kooky things like Creationism, the Great Flood, or that the Devil was thrown out of heaven in the 20th Century

(signaling the start of the End Times) have about an 8th grade education and live in Hillbilly Town, Kentucky. (Sorry for that long sentence, Danny.)

4. I want 8th graders all across the country to read it, give up on their faith, and get sent to religion-based boot camps by frightened parents who don't understand them and think they're possessed by demons.

I've always fancied myself a cartoonist. Above and beyond being a writer, sculptor, screenwriter, ladies-only exotic dancer, and fashion model for plus size men's bowling shirts, I'm a doodler at heart. When I'm in a meeting, I doodle. I turn my to-do lists into to-doodle lists. When I am finding a solution to a problem, I sketch it out with doodles. When I write a love letter, it's usually punctuated with a doodle. A doodle is an informal drawing, falling somewhere on the illustration scale between a cartoon and a coffee stain on a napkin. It usually lacks depth, effort, or skill.

The Illustration Scale							
		✓					
Coffee Stain	Stick Figure	Doodle	Cartoon	Technical Illustration	Formal Art	Bob Ross	Masterpiece

Doodling is the kind of manual exercise anyone who can scratch lines on paper can perform, despite their skill level or artistry. So this book is full of my doodles.

I think people who belong to cults or people who believe in the literal translation of the Bible have been brainwashed. (You know who you are.) You operate on auto-pilot and are controlled by fear. Brainwashing is all about procedure, repetition, and reinforcement (usually negative reinforcement). Think of any church service, mass, or call to prayer you've attended and how structured and repetitive they have been.

So, to help you face your fears, I've added a "Doodle Time" section to many of the chapters of this book, where I encourage you to draw something funny about a topic being discussed or about something you've been taught to take very serious.

Each Doodle Time section will have instructions of what to draw and tips on how to make it interesting or funny. This is great for those times in Bible study class when the teacher is droning on and on about who begat whom and how long those old farts lived. Pull out this book and start doodling. It will help you laugh at the things you've been brainwashed to think are sacred. Plus, it will help you overcome your fear of defacing a book. Deface away! Your third grade librarian had a stick up her butt.

Each Doodle Time section will have this header:

Doodle Time:

and might have some dots to connect, doodles already partially drawn, or backgrounds filled in. Some chapters have extra, bonus Doodle Times for your drawing, anti-brainwashing pleasure.

Sharpen that #2 pencil or get that pen out, and keep it handy while you read because I'll call on you often to use it. If I'm going to hell for doodling, I might as well drag you there with me.

About religion

Throughout this manual I mention that I don't care what people believe. I think everybody has the right to worship anyone and any way they want. I do not think religion is bad. Nor do I think it is inherently evil or corrupt. There is a reason religion exists in every culture across the globe. It is a natural occurrence in society, just as sports competitions, police forces, and mimes naturally occur. That's not to say that I don't think mimes are inherently evil and corrupt. Nothing says "evil corruption" quite like a mime. He just says it very very quietly.

Religion provides hope

There's no question about that. Hope for an afterlife; hope for a release from the sadness, pain, and suffering we all endure in this world at one time or another; and hope for justice on the unjust. The latter is the promise that the universe is a fair and ultimately good place, which may or may not be true. And by providing hope, religion brings comfort to our otherwise less-than-comforting lives. It may be false hope but a little comfort and encouragement makes you feel good.

I think it's a neat little tool, religion. It's our household multi-purpose gadget that we use to fix things in our lives. It lifts us up when we're depressed. Comforts us in time of need. It holds out the promise that all this effort is for something. Something good. And it prevents us from doing "bad" things. Well, it prevents some of us from doing some bad things. Better put, it keeps us from doing the worst things, and hopefully makes us think twice about doing things that are a little bad. Either way, it's still a tool. It's just the right tool for the right problem. Trouble starts, though, when we use our tool to fix something in someone else's house.

Some would say religion is our relationship with God, but I disagree. I think a person can have a personal relationship with whatever he or she considers divine without getting religion involved. I call that spirituality. The conversation you have with Him, Her, or It is private, whether that is praying, meditating, or staring at a sunset. If you have a conversation with God and He talks to you, can anyone else hear what He's saying? No. So why should your side of the conversation be anything but just as silent? That relationship, your spirituality, is a driving force that keeps you happy, helps you make choices in your life, and steers you away from the evil and corrupt mimes of the world.

Sometimes when I see people saying grace in restaurants I can tell right away who the leader is. Subtle body language, like whose hand is on top (if they're holding hands), who is saying the grace, and if the other person is fidgety or nervous, gives me a Jim Jones shiver.

I don't think there has to be any organization to the time or method in which you commune with God, nature, or your left shoe. There don't need to be rules. Or better yet, if you think there should be rules about how and when you commune with the hosts of heaven, go ahead and practice them, but don't worry about how anybody else is doing it. Why do you have to say grace right before you eat a meal? Why not say grace when you're cooking? That might prevent more accidents in the kitchen. Or what about when you go to a restaurant? Could a prayer in the parking lot be a better way of thanking the Almighty for the dining experi-

Bad, dogma. Bad!

Saint Nauseum of Condemnia abuses his dancing weiners for not saying grace before dinner.

ence of which you are about to partake, rather than waiting until the food is placed before you? Your chances for good service might improve.

If you and I sit down for a meal and you pause to say grace out loud before you eat and I don't, how do you know I haven't already said a silent prayer over the food? Does it really matter? I don't think it's disrespectful to start eating while you're thanking God for the food. You should give me the benefit of the doubt and assume that God and I have an arrangement that precludes letting the food get cold before diving into it.

Like I said, I don't think spirituality, religion, or believing in the supernatural is bad. I think the human element, people, has a corrupting effect on all endeavors, and religion is not immune to this influence. As soon as you try to define a feeling, put it in a box, and give it a name, you open the door for someone else to disagree with you. That's when they will try to define their feeling about the same thing by putting it in a slightly different box with a different name. Before you know it, you'll have a dozen boxes with a dozen names, and a dozen people saying their box holds the truth while your box and all the others are meant to mislead people.

So, before long, you start asking other people to decide whose definition about this feeling is correct, and to someone's dismay, one box is chosen over eleven others. And guess what? Your box wasn't the lucky winner. So what do you do? You disagree with the selection and set out to destroy the others. But, to achieve this goal, you need someone to lead you.

I think we've learned throughout history that as soon as someone is in charge, all bets are off. The original goal nearly always migrates toward the benefit of those in charge. We elect a politician or follow a revolutionary leader with the lofty, honorable goal of cleaning up the government or overthrowing tyranny, but when he's done with **that task, he typically becomes the thing he was sent to destroy.**

Ask yourself something: is someone in charge of your church? Does it have a governing body, a council, or some organization that makes administrative decisions? Are they necessary? Do they decide which hymnals you use, which prayers are said, or how you take communion? Do they have the authority to kick you out of the church?

That's not religion, that's *organized* religion. The real enemy.

Religion gives hope, comfort and order. As long as you use religion to guide your own life and not someone else's, you're in the safe zone. Unfortunately, too many people use religion to try to control the lives of other people. And that's why I distrust it.

That's what I believe. It's baseless and lacks any proof, fact, or historical documentation. It comes from deep inside my brain, where it has lots of room to rattle around, all alone in there with nothing but a couple of girlie pictures on one gray, wrinkled wall, and ELO's greatest hits playing over and over again.

You don't need to debate a feeling you have inside. It's how you feel and it's up to you to explore that feeling, flesh it out and call it pumpkin pie. You don't need me to give you ammunition in a battle that can't be won.

And if you're born again, keep it to yourself. Let's say I experience a fantastic movie or read a phenomenal book. No, let's stick with the movie, since that's more realistic for me. I see a movie that changes my life. Why should I share the news with friends, and encourage them over and over to watch the movie hoping it will be as life-changing for them as it was for me? I shouldn't fool myself into thinking it's going to have the exact same impact on them. And the next day when I see my friends and ask them what they thought of the movie, they'll probably shrug and say, "eh, it was OK." Why should I argue that it's the greatest movie ever made and that they should tell everyone they know to watch it? Why should I expect them to be in the exact same place in their life that I was in my life when I saw it and expect them to react the same way?

What I should do, is tell them I liked it, recommend it as worthy of the ticket price, and let them decide if it's any good or even if they want to go see it. I shouldn't burden them with the threat of a life less lived because they haven't seen the movie.

We shouldn't be talking about who believes what. My beliefs are mine and I'll do what I want with them. Now, if my beliefs were to trespass on someone else's rights or liberties, such as eating babies or redirecting traffic into a lake, then maybe they should be up for debate. And then maybe we should define their value in our society. For example, there are some beliefs that encroach on others' rights, such as oppressing people based on their gender or race. That's the kind of thing we should be talking about.

Who owns the Bible?

For legal reasons, I need to make a copyright acknowledgement, but thought it a good time to bring something to your attention. In preparation for writing this book, I researched religious articles, encyclopedias, the Sunday funnies and I reviewed many passages from several Holy Bibles, such as the King James Version and the NIV. It has come to my attention that some of these texts (or translations) are actually copyrighted by their publishers. For example, the NIV, the New International Version of the Bible is owned by a company called Zondervan, and copyrighted by the International Bible Society. Their website clearly spells out how to acknowledge quotes from their translation of the Bible and what the legal obligations are for anyone with the intent of using their works for commercial or non-commercial use.

This book is obviously a for-commercial endeavor. Since it's a confession rather than a commentary or Bible reference, I have used fewer than 500 verses, and the verses I used do not account for 25% of the total text, all I am obligated to do is include the appropriate copyright acknowledgement, which is:

If you believe in God, search your heart and ask yourself if He thinks it's OK for someone to say they "own" the Holy Bible.

Whose bone am I picking?

Some people think I have a bone to pick with people of faith, the church or God. They think I'm angry at God, or was abused by a priest when I was an altar boy and am taking it out on religion. Some think that I prayed for something really hard for many years, like winning the lottery, and am angry at the universe for not letting me win. Well, the last one holds a little truth, but the rest isn't true.

The bone I have to pick is with people who believe in the literal interpretation of the Bible (or any holy book), the people who spread this way of thinking, those who use it to frighten and control their communities, and those who believe it's sinful to exercise your brain by asking simple questions about the nature of the universe.

For example, if you think I am going to literally burn in a lake of fire for all eternity while fanged demons devour my flesh for the following cartoon[1], then the bone I have to pick is with you.

Oh, Simon, my bronze-shouldered fisherman, how I yearned to wrestle thee. Now that dream will never be.

I think Jesus was gay.

---

1   For more thoughts about this cartoon, see notes on it at the end of this book.

If you go to church on Sunday, denouncing vice and immorality, then have sex with your neighbor's wife on Monday, I have a bone to pick with you. I despise religious hypocrites even more than I dislike intolerant fanatics.

Test your literalism

Grab that #2 pencil! Here's your first test. Answer Yes or No to these statements to see if you are a Biblical literalist or not. None of the answers should require any extra explanations or qualifications. In your opinion, these things are either true or not, without symbolism or metaphor.

Yes   No

☐   ☐   God created Adam out of dust (or clay) and then made Eve from one of Adam's ribs.

☐   ☐   Jesus Christ resurrected Lazarus from the dead.

☐   ☐   God flooded the Earth by causing it to rain 40 days and 40 nights, and Noah saved all the animals of the world by putting them in his boat.

☐   ☐   After teaching one afternoon, Jesus fed over 5,000 people with 5 loaves of bread and 2 fish.

☐   ☐   God destroyed the cities of Sodom and Gomorrah with fire and brimstone from heaven.

☐   ☐   Lot's wife was turned into a pillar of salt for looking back at the destruction of Sodom as they fled the city.

☐   ☐   The Rapture will occur one day, at which time Christians will vanish from the Earth and be transported to heaven.

☐   ☐   Lucifer (the Devil) lives in Hell and commands legions of demons to do his bidding (like causing temptation and possessing politicians, preachers and little girls).

Don't take that test out of context. If you believe in that stuff, I don't want you to stop. I just want you to examine yourself and to be self-aware, so that we both know what side of the fence we're on. If you're a religious person, I don't want to beat you over the head with my antichrist stick. My goal isn't to convert you away from your belief system, just to explain mine. Of course, part of explaining my beliefs is to tell you why I think you're wrong and why I think your religion is false and deceitful. Whack, whack, whack. But don't take it as an attack or an insult. Whack. Accept my argument as the God's honest truth. You accepted what they told you in Sunday school, right? What's the difference? Whack whack.

If you said you believe some of the things in that test but not all of them, ask yourself why. What's the difference? What makes one story from the Bible true and something else just a fairy tale? That's one of the reasons I'm an Atheist. It's obvious to me that most of those stories are just made up.

Why do I laugh at religion?

Not that religion is the slightest bit humorous. And it's not that I don't take it serious. I take it very serious. Religion is a dangerous thing. Very dangerous. I've pondered it and questioned my position for decades.

I use humor for two reasons. First, because being irreverent shows religion that I'm not afraid of it. Second, because life is short. One day you're hiking to the top of Pikes Peak without a care in the world and the next day they're burying your cold, lifeless body in a box. Please don't bury me in a silk-lined casket that costs more than a used car. A plain, pine box, or better yet, a really REALLY hot fire (if you're absolutely certain I'm dead) is all I need to put me to rest, thank you very much.

Zarry

Prologue

*Z*arry sat on the hewn stone table, beyond the edge of the muted sunlight seeping in from the entryway. Through the loose knit of his new wool robe, the smooth rock was cold against his thighs. He absently swung his legs, rapping the heels of his sandals rhythmically against the rough-sided pedestal, and hugged the cloth satchel on his lap to his chest. The quiet darkness of his tomb did not comfort him.

It was a stupid nickname. He picked it when he was a child, and it never stuck. No one in his family called him Zarry despite years of insistence by him that they should. He had no friends, beyond the occasional business acquaintance, and they would not use it. One childhood companion had called him Laz for a week and then Zar for a few years. He smiled at the thought of them playing together on their way to temple. But the smile faded at the image of his friend, whose name he couldn't remember, donkey cart piled high with belongings, leaving Bethany as his family moved north of Tyre to work in the olive orchards. No one else had called him Laz or Zar and no one had ever called him Zarry. He gave up on the nickname six months after his wedding.

The wedding had been arranged by his mother. And despite promises that his bride would learn to love him, that the spark of physical intimacy would grow into a flame of passion, there was never a spark to light the fire. His wife had as much interest in matters of the flesh as she might have in plucking a chicken. It was a sticky chore to perform without enthusiasm, followed by a hot bath to wash off the stink of wet feathers. They had nothing in common. She was older than him by a few years, some would say past her prime, which is why her family settled for a merchant's bookkeeper as her husband, far from their home town, he thought.

Zarry's wife was a Pharisee, angry and proud, who frowned on living away from the sea. She followed the letter of the

Law, every consonant, and ignored the spirit of its meaning. "Parables," she often said, "are for dreamers and Galileans with too much time on their hands." She was an immaculate housekeeper who kept their home spotless and sparse. He was, well, Zarry was just Zarry. Neither a zealot, nor an unreligious man, he tithed at the temple and obeyed the laws of the Sabbath. Once a year he paid the rabbi for a blessing on his home in the hopes that his wife would bear him a child. But he knew in his heart that her clenched disinterest strangled his seed before it could find fertile soil. If he ever prayed it was to be crushed in the street by a runaway legionnaire's chariot, thus ending his miserable existence. In fact, he often walked down the center of the busiest street of Bethany on his way to and from the market, hoping that around the corner or on some unnoticed side street a Roman soldier's horse was about to be spooked by a stray dog or a horsefly and come hurtling out of nowhere. During temple services, while the men prayed around him, Zarry hummed quietly to allow his mind to wander. When he slept, he dreamed of being an empty boat untethered from the dock, drifting lazily on the smooth windless surface of a lake. When he looked up at the sky, he never felt like anyone was looking back down at him. He found no solace in his wife's stony presence. He often mused that he knew exactly what it would have been like if Lot had stayed behind with his wife after she had been turned into a pillar of salt.

He had always been lonely, though rarely alone. His mother and older sisters, Martha and Mary, were permanent fixtures in his life. They made his affairs their business, criticizing and nitpicking every decision he ever made. They poured cold water on every dream he had until life was nothing more than the ledger upon which he catalogued his days along with the grain and salt he purchased in the market for his Roman merchant employer. And with his wife, they crushed his manhood with snide words of discouragement and harsh judgment.

In the darkness, Zarry wondered how long it would take for him to die. The idea had come to him one day in the market after he had stared at the brown, weather-beaten face of a wool merchant for an hour, wondering if the wrinkled old man had saved enough money to be buried in a proper tomb, or if he would spend eternity staring up at tree roots from a pauper's grave. He fixated on the thought of his own tomb and how peaceful it would be to lie inside. Six months later the land was purchased, the excavation complete, his family name was carved over the entry, and he sat on the slab dangling his legs and dreading the voice that would call to him from the sunlit cemetery outside.

"Husband?"

He cringed at the sound of his wife's voice and wrinkled his nose. She had been trying to coax him out of the tomb for three days now. He was missing a full day before she even noticed his absence. On the second day Zarry wrapped his arms and head with funerary cloth in case the urge to shuffle off his mortal coil came upon him suddenly or in case he died in his sleep. How long does it take to die? He was certain that four days without real food would kill him. Wasn't it popular belief these days that a man cannot live on bread alone? He pulled the last loaf of sesame seed bread from his satchel and eyed it suspiciously, then tossed it on the floor beside the half-full goatskin of water. What does modern science know? I should have stuck with just water.

"Husband." She was losing patience.

"Zarry!" he called toward the light. "It's Zarry!"

"My husband," she responded coolly, as if to a belligerent child. He could tell she was shaking her head dismissively. She had never called him by his given name, not in the privacy of their home, and not even if she yelled to him from across a crowded street. Their marriage was a contract between families and she carried it as such, a business arrangement. If it didn't sound disrespectful she would have called him mister husband. "It's time to come out."

"Leave me alone," he called, "I'm dying, here!" He didn't fear being forcibly removed from his tomb. The people of his village were far too superstitious to set foot inside the grave of a man that wasn't dead, even more so afraid of the tomb of a crazy person. His wife couldn't bear to even stand on the steps leading up to the entrance. She positioned herself off the funerary path in the shade of the olive tree he had paid the grave diggers to plant outside the entry. He chose the olive tree in memory of the nameless friend who had come close to calling him Zarry.

"I've sent word to your sisters. They're coming to help."

Great. Just great. I'm doomed. His plan had been to end it all while his sisters were out of town. If they returned they would team up with his wife and nag him out of his tomb. The three of them could take eight-hour shifts and verbally abuse him twenty-four hours a day. He'd never get any sleep, except maybe on the Sabbath. He wasn't sure if they considered nagging work or play. But as much time and energy they devoted to it, he was sure he could argue the point with a rabbi, and at least get one day of rest a week, if it came to that.

"Husband," her voice was lowered and he had to strain to hear her through the funerary wrappings over his ears, "a crowd is gathering. This could be embarrassing."

"For who, you?" he called from the darkness, "I'm dead. I don't have a worry in the world!"

"Husband, I know you've been depressed at work lately --"

"Zarry!"

"Husband --"

"Zarry! Call me Zarry and I'll come out." He was resolute. For all his death-wishing, if he could convince her to give in just this once, then there was the tiniest promise that he could find happiness in the world. If he could convince her to bend a tiny bit, he might consider bending himself and the two of them might learn to compromise. "Come on," he called, "just one little word."

Silence fell. He could almost hear the grinding of her teeth and the wet-fingers-on-polished-marble squeak of the pursing of her lips as the battle raged within her.

"My husband," she began.

"Stubborn cow!" Zarry said to himself, ignoring whatever she was saying. Maybe some Roman guards will come to investigate the crowd, mark him as a troublemaker, and run him through with a spear! The thought intrigued him and filled him with a sudden hope, except for the running through part. What does it take to get killed by a Roman guard? Defame the emperor, or somehow publicly question his divine ancestry. He shook his head, certain the plan would backfire on him. Before killing him the Romans would make an example of him for insulting the emperor, probably by feeding him to lions or beating him senseless. It would be a long, drawn-out public affair. Then, after his suffering and humiliation had driven him to the very edge of death, they would kill him as a final punishment. Far too dreadful for his tastes. He preferred to die of starvation in the cool shade of his tomb.

He could hear the crowd now. The hum of twenty or thirty unintelligible voices crept into the tomb and annoyed him. He was about to shout that they were making enough noise to wake the dead when his blood froze. Over the monotone droning of the crowd he could hear his sister, Martha, calling to his wife. Like suddenly biting into a wormy nut after eating a handful of sweet choice pistachios, his mouth went dry and he reached for the goatskin to wash the bitter taste out of his mouth.

Martha was the worst of his sisters. She never talked, she only screeched. Her voice was that of a pet monkey from Cush being skinned alive, splitting the air with blood-curdling precision. He cringed at the sound of her shrieking his wife's name, no doubt as she bullied her way through the crowd with his other sister, Mary, in tow.

Mary was slow-witted and fat. But neither in a good way. She followed Martha's example as they grew up, verbally abusing Zarry and degrading him at every opportunity until he cringed in her presence as much as he cringed at Martha's voice or his mother's disappointed stare. Mary never married and was easily outwitted by opportunistic men, and thus had gained the reputation of a woman of loose morals. Her slow-wittedness and the threat of being accosted by her harpy of a sister saved her from being labeled a whore and stoned to death. Recently she had taken the company of a traveling mystic, serving him and his entourage as cook, cleaner and bath maid.

The three women jabbered outside his tomb as his wife explained the situation and his sisters howled with shrill disapproval. He could hear them lamenting that the family's honor was at risk and their insistence that they would do everything in their means to bring him out.

Zarry shuddered at the thought and lay back on the cold stone. He stared into the darkness above him and wondered if he could cause the limestone roof to collapse upon him by sheer strength of will. He counted his heartbeats for a few minutes then breathed a heavy sigh and steeled himself to walk out of the tomb, head low, to face the wrath that awaited him outside. He took another swig of water from the goatskin, his last taste of the sweet freedom of death, then dropped it on the tomb floor and sat up.

Just then the crowd went silent, even his wife and sisters grew quiet. One voice, too far and low for him to make out, was addressing them. The Romans, he realized. The local captain of the guard was probably inquiring on the commotion before he ordered the crowd to disperse, and Mary answered him belligerently, almost like she was berating him.

Fool! She would be his undoing. The crowd had drawn the Roman guards' attention but the subsequent wrath brought down upon him would be the work of his stupid sister. He began planning an exit strategy, wondering if he could slip out of the tomb while their collective attentions were on the soldiers.

The captain's voice moved closer to the entrance as he spoke and Zarry realized that he didn't have a Roman accent. It was the mystic, Jeshua, for whom Mary cooked and cleaned. A Galilean carpenter-turned-soothsayer who touted the fundamentals of the Law in one hand while promoting the concept of salvation here on Earth in the other, Jeshua had built a small group of faithful followers who traveled with him from city to city, looking for handouts, arguing with the teachers in the temple, and speaking in parables. He had made a name for himself as a comical nuisance while his motley crew of fisherman, laborers, husbandless women and disenfranchised city clerks treated him like some high ranking diplomatic emmisary from a kingdom no one had heard of before.

Zarry had met Jeshua once a few months ago, just after Mary joined his traveling band. She brought them to Bethany to eat his food, tell **riddle-like stories that made no sense to a wine-addled** mind, and to ask Zarry to help finance their mission to build a new temple. He would have thrown the smelly lot of them out of his house if their presence hadn't so upset his orthodox wife.

A murmur ran through the crowd as Jeshua rebuked Mary for her belligerence. Zarry smiled. You get her, Jesh. Teach her who's boss. He reclined on the stone again and thought that he might be able to stay.

Jeshua was known for giving passionate speeches that raised the blood pressure of his followers. They would dance through the crowds of local onlookers, cheer him and sing his praises, then canvas the locals for donations and a home where they could throw a party at the host's expense. Therein laid Zarry's escape from his wife and sisters. There were no hosts to be found in the graveyard. If Jeshua's speech was followed by a party, the whole crowd would have to move to it, leaving the graveyard, his tomb, and his pride intact and taking at least one if his sisters with them. He crossed his arms and smiled at the dark ceiling. All I have to do is wait.

"Lazarus!"

The voice echoed into Zarry's tomb and hung about him. His smile faded as he realized that this wasn't a sermon, it was an intervention.

"Lazarus, rise from the darkness."

Zarry had forgotten how hypnotic Jeshua could be when he focused his attention on you. He hopped off the table and began pacing, circling his funerary dais. Damn, damn, damn!

"Rise, Lazarus! Your time among the living is not over!"

Third time's the charm, Zarry thought. The next thing Jeshua is going to say is, "don't make me come in there," and then I'll be a laughing stock as well as humiliated. He kicked the goatskin against the wall and trundled up the steps toward the entrance.

Grabbing the stone cap he had used to partially barricade the tomb entrance, he heaved it aside. The warm setting sun struck his face through the thin burial gauze, and he raised an arm to shield his eyes.

The crowd gasped and backed away. Children screamed and women swooned. A panic swelled in the crowd, threatening to explode with a rush, either away in all directions or toward Zarry in horrified violence.

Jeshua calmed them with a word and coaxed them forward. He emplored them to embrace Zarry, to help him remove his funerary **bandages, and see that he was no walking corpse. They came** forward in pairs at first, squeezing Zarry's arms and touching his face to feel the warmth of life. Then the whole group mobbed him with concern.

Confused by the care this crowd showed him and the lack of ridicule, Zarry stood in their midst and let them peel away the cotton strips and his new wool robe. The sun was warm on his body and Jeshua's dancing girls seemed less wanton and more free-spirited and angelic than he remembered.

One of Jeshua's followers, a tall man with smiling eyes wrapped the robe back around Zarry's naked body and thumped him heartily on the back. "Welcome back," he said, "where's the party?"

"My house," Zarry responded without even thinking. He glanced to the shade of the olive tree where his wife and sisters spoke with Jeshua. His wife pressed a coin sack into Jeshua's palm and it deftly disappeared into his robe.

Zarry smiled and laughed out loud while the crowd continued to fawn over him, moving en masse out of the graveyard, into town toward his house. He felt like a new man.

Resurrected.

Breaking the news to your parents

Chapter 1

Breaking the news of your recently found Atheism to your parents can be difficult. If they're good parents, they've paid attention to you growing up and have guided you away from the dumb choices you often wanted to make. They know your hot buttons and weak spots. They fear for your eternal soul and can talk you out of anything.

For starters, avoid dropping the big bomb on them during dinner one night, the way you told them you crossed state lines to pay for an abortion after asking for another slice of vegetarian pizza. You need to be more subtle.

Ask them if they ever had doubts about God's existence when they were kids. Not only will this show them that you're interested in hearing stories about their life experiences, it also primes the pump for lessening their concerns. When you tell them you don't think God is real, they will rationalize away any fears that you're making a colossal mistake by thinking you're just having the same doubts they had at your age, and that they will pass the same way their doubts passed. They won't realize that you're well past the doubt stage and into the full-fledged denial stage.

If God doesn't exist, then how did religion first start?

As I mentioned before, religion provides hope. There's no question about that. Hope for an afterlife; hope for a release from the sadness, pain, and suffering we all endure at one time or another in this world; and hope for justice on the unjust. That last part is the promise that the universe is a fair and ultimately good place. We encounter the unfairness of the universe every day. We hear about murders and theft. We see other people get away with endangering lives by running red lights, while we get tickets for the victimless crime of having a crack in our windshield. (Did you read that, Officer Templeton? I said it's unfair to hand out tickets for cracked windshields when other people are running red lights.) We need to know deep down inside that the unfairness we witness is the exception and that the "bad guy" will get his in the end. Religion provides that Hollywood ending to us and brings comfort to our otherwise less-than-comforting lives.

I think religion started with a lion.

Lions are nocturnal hunters. That means they're sneaky bastards who go for your jugular after you have settled in for the evening. They're like telemarketers at the end of the twentieth century.

When we were hunter-gatherers, living in the fields, we had to compete for food resources and we had to watch our backs because we were someone else's source of food. I say "hunter-gatherers, living in fields," because the Creationists would get all riled-up if I said "cavemen." I don't know if it offends their sense of cleanliness, the thought of people living in a cave, bat guano under their toenails, and rocks for pillows, or if they think it is an affront to God for people to use naturally occurring shelters to protect themselves from His fury, instead of building shabby huts out of mud and twigs.

By the way, "guano" is a funny sounding name for feces, excrement, pooh, caca. It's found in caves and is typically reserved for bats, so you'll never hear a naturalist refer to bison guano. Please don't mail me any. I use the term for two reasons. First, to avoid offending the readers who think the word "shit" is any more crude or offensive than the word "dookie." Second, because I mentioned Creationists in the same paragraph, and I know in my heart that if I used the term "bat shit" in conjunction with the word "Creationist," no one would take me seriously. Especially after they applied the Bible Code[1] to my book and determined that I was a religion-basher, bent on libeling a particular sect.

Back to the lion story. When we were field-dwelling hunter-gatherers, we hunted in the fields, we gathered in the fields, we ate in the fields, made baby hunter-gatherers in the fields, and we slept in the fields. Except, it was a restless sleep. It was restless because of the lions.

They were out there, beyond the light of our campfires, watching us. They watched us a lot back then because they were just as smart as us, and they knew that if they were patient, one of us would eventually stroll out of the protective ring of firelight to make pee-pee and fall prey to their waiting claws and fangs. In the middle of the night, nothing tastes as good to a lion as a human with a full bladder. Without horns and hooves, and with only a soft, paper-thin hide, **nabbing a human is like plucking a ripe peach from a tree**.

They don't watch us like that anymore. Now we're smarter than the lions. We have Land Rovers and stiff-sided tents with chemical toi-

---

1   The Bible Code is a mathematical method for finding "secret" messages and prophecies in the Bible, hidden there by God. Read the books, they're a hoot. The rule for using the Bible Code conveniently lets them skip forward when necessary or pick letters in such a way that they build fairly complex sentences. But it makes no sense and doesn't explain why God or whoever inserted the code into the Bible would care about things like the Twin Towers being destroyed or that a comet collided with Jupiter (affecting nothing here on Earth).

lets. And we have the great equalizer, the gun. But they're patient, and for now they'll let us bask in our dominion over the creatures of the fields and forests. They're biding their time in their zoos and animal preserves. "One day," they say at the monthly lion's club meeting, "man will get complacent and he'll forget his chemical toilet at the other camp and have to stroll into the darkness to make pee-pee."

So we were afraid. At first, we were afraid of the watcher in the darkness. We were afraid of its terrible power and its hunger to take us away. Then we became afraid of the darkness itself, because that was where the danger laid in wait. The darkness represented more than just the lion; it represented the unknown and it represented our own mortality, the inevitability of death.

Nothing tastes as good to a lion as a human with a full bladder

The fear of the dark unknown evolved into superstition. I don't mean the constant sophisticated-but-trivial superstition of today where we knock on wood so as to block potentially jinxing[2] ourselves, or tossing a pinch of spilled salt over our shoulder, but a more primitive superstition. It was the superstition of survival.

Since almost every animal we hunted was bigger, stronger and faster than us, or at least the ones worth hunting to feed a whole tribe, and also because the animals that hunted us were bigger, stronger and faster than us, we needed an edge – or – more of an edge than sharpened sticks and broken rocks. Call it confidence, or bravery, or dumb luck, but the edge we needed to succeed was found in the form of a little thing called a talisman.

---

2   Jinx: the act of invoking bad luck upon oneself, usually through stating a fact. "I've never had a speeding ticket," "luckily, I've never been audited," and, "I've never been sick a day in my life," are all jinx-invoking statements. To magically prevent the jinx, you need simply knock on bare wood with your knuckles. If no bare wood is present, you can knock on anything resembling wood, as long as you say, "knock on wood," while doing it. I'm not sure how quickly the jinx-blocking magic has to be performed after the jinx statement is made, but I'm sure it's pretty darn quick. Which supernatural entity actually causes the curse to take place? It could be God, the devil, or pixies in the pantry, but no one is certain.

Perhaps the very first religious ceremony was to rub a little strip of bear fur against the sharp end of a spear in the hopes that some of the dead bear's spirit would enter the weapon and make the spear kill its prey on the first throw.

We learned early on that death could also drive death away. The big hunters were smart enough to fear their own dead. We picked up on that and started wearing their pelts like clothing. Anthropologists and sociologists might argue that human hunters wore the hides of animal hunters to gain strength from that animal's spirit, but I think that's more advanced than the very first and simplest emotion. The hunter who killed a lion would wear the lion's hide to say, "Look what I did!" and "Watch your step! You're trespassing on dangerous territory!" It was a warning to other lions, and most definitely a warning to other hunters. We're all about having a pecking order, now as much as then.

Some anthropologists might assert that we more likely wore the hides of herd animals that we killed than our predators' hides so that we could run amongst them for ambushes and to get the most entertainment out of the psychedelic mushrooms we stumbled upon. But despite my lack of education on the subject, I think that came much later. Protection against the enemy came before the strategies of hunting. Can you imagine how delightful a human in a fur coat would seem to a lion surveying a herd of water buffalo? "Hey, Herb," one lion would say to another, "look at that water buffalo with only two legs. Not only is he crippled, he's also slower than the other herd members, and his legs are bare and hoofless, like those hairless meat bags we munch on for midnight snacks. Let's take him down." Not a very effective defense. But shaking a dead lion pelt at a pride of lions would make them think twice.

So we used fear as a weapon and as a talisman of protection. The lion's fear of our lion-skin hunting attire and our campfires, was powerful magic. We didn't understand psychology. All we knew was that the symbol worked, and that gave it power. When we didn't keep the fire burning all night, or when we hunted without our lion-skin robe, a hungry lion nabbed someone. It was cause-and-effect learning. So we expanded the symbolism to other objects and other aspects of life. A necklace of dried berries and husks helped the gatherer find more berry bushes. A tent or robe sewn with a fishbone needle was more likely to keep out the rain. We began to rely on our talismans.

At some point we learned how to express these thoughts and feelings through art. People would gather in the cave and marvel at the murals that were painted. The first cave painting was probably a depiction of an historical event. Looking at a cave painting of a great hunt helped the hunters remember their successes and gave them confidence. That confidence was more magic we didn't understand. Hunters who didn't dance under the bearskin robe around the fire, or those who didn't journey into the cave to review the game plan painted on the wall, didn't do as well in the field. They didn't have the magical confidence that they gained from the drawings and the talismans. Pretty soon, they couldn't have one without the other.

As animals, our first big step was that we became self-aware. Somewhere between pure survival instinct and developing the language and social rules of group dynamics, we realized our own mortality. We learned that we grew old and died if something didn't eat us first, and we learned how to fear death. Animals that aren't self-aware don't fear death; they fear the things that cause death.

Our instincts naturally herded us into family groups, which became communities, which became tribes of communities. We started to learn more about ourselves, just through proximity, and the world around us, which up until that point was new to us every day. And since we didn't understand much about how things worked (like weather, seasons, and menstruation) we became even more superstitious.

River valley dwellers developed a whole range of superstitions surrounding the needs and dangers of living near a river. Rains caused floods, after all, and as hard as it is to believe, we couldn't explain them. Drought diminished the river's bounty, another natural event we couldn't explain and couldn't control. We found that wearing the lion-skin robe and shaking our bear-blessed spear at the river wouldn't make it rise. But, if we danced for days and days and burned great stacks of wood to make clouds, rain would come, eventually. Sure, it was coincidence that during a drought in most fertile river valleys, if you wait long enough it will eventually rain, or the snow in the mountains will eventually begin to melt, and the river will rise. But we didn't know that was how it worked. We only knew that our superstitions were a necessary magic, and we had to believe that they worked, otherwise everyday magic, like knowing that a lion-skin robe will keep the lions from eating you, would be worthless and the great and powerful hunters and gatherers we had become would be thrown back into the world of being flat-toothed, clawless, hide-less chimps who were only able to survive through luck and a little ingenuity.

I have a simple formula for the evolution of religion. It starts with superstition and ends with organized religion, and it looks something like this:

Self-awareness	+ Fear	= Superstition	
Superstition	+ Community	= Religion	
Religion	+ Politics	= Organized Religion	

The human condition naturally leans toward tribalism. Our self-perception and our definition of everything in our environment revolve around the need to categorize and find patterns. For example, I don't look for toilet paper on the canned vegetable aisle at the grocery store. I look for it in the paper products aisle, or perhaps on the end of an aisle if it's on sale. Categories have patterns.

The fundamental superstitions we developed in the early stages were carried up into the new communities, but each community developed its own new and specialized superstitions to meet the growing needs of the community. And with community living, we started to learn about RULES.

Rule Number 1: Don't kill each other.

Tricked you. If you're thinking, "Thou shalt not kill," was one of the early rules, you're wrong. The concept of making a rule that says, "Don't murder each other," most likely came pretty late in the rule making game. Actually, rule number one was probably "Be quiet." We were hunter-gatherers, after all. In order to hunt our prey, which could run faster than us, fly, or could stomp our heads in if it knew we were coming, we had to be able to sneak up on it. Similarly, when we were gathering stuff in the fields, we had to be quiet in order to keep from attracting things that would munch on our tender parts.

Rule Number 1 (Revised): Be Quiet.

"But when we go hiking in the national park, they say we should make noise by talking and whistling, to warn bears and mountain lions of our presence so they can hide from us." Sure, that's something we do today because the tables have turned and those predators know what's good for them. But back when the sounds of us chirping and squawking was like ringing the dinner bell, we learned pretty quickly that those who like to sing in the fields were those who didn't live past the ripe old age of fourteen. Plus, here's a test you can take: go up into grizzly bear regions of Alaska or the Yukon by yourself, wander around in the backcountry and gather berries and flowers along the way. Occasionally whistle a snappy tune and don't try to hide from that big Kodiak when he comes lumbering along to see what's making all that noise in his berry field. You'll see how quickly those rules about making noise apply, and also how easy it is to reduce our gene pool by one.

Rule Number 2: Do what the Leader Says.

Humans naturally fall into two categories: leaders and followers. In that regard we're just like wolves, dogs, and herd animals. You have an alpha male, an alpha female, and then you have everybody else. There are all kinds of studies on the psychological and chemical ballet of group dynamics, but it basically comes down to this: if there is more than one person working toward a goal, they will unconsciously select a leader, a leader will consciously assume the role, or the whole group will divide into smaller groups, each with a leader, and fight it out.

Try to play an imagination game with a six-year-old. They almost always assume the role of leadership and tell you what your make-believe role will be. "No, Uncle Thom, you're the dinosaur. *I'm* the spaceman."

So, how does the leader get the people to do what he wants? He applies brute force and reminds his community that might makes right. "Do what I say or I'll bash your head in." Since some people are natural leaders and some people are natural followers, this phrase can be expanded to, "Do what I say or one of my followers will bash your head in."

To give you an idea of how basic these rules are, assume that these statements were being made in a time before we actually had a spoken language. I'm talking about tens of thousands of years ago. The only language we understood were the grunts, exclamations, and coos that only meant something when used in combination with actions and emotions. "Do what I say or I'll bash your head in," was probably accomplished with a growl and a push, or maybe a snarl and poke with a sharp stick.

Since this book is about religion and not language, I'll skip forward a few thousand years to when we had fairly robust vocabularies.

Once we finally had words, we used them to describe the world around us. We used words to tell the stories we had painted on the cave walls. And we finally had a word for our greatest fear: death. Along with the word for death came the words for the other things we couldn't see but were certain existed. We gave names to the magic we knew was in things, the mojo that made things work.

Spoken language brought with it layers of complexity for our communities and our superstitions. Concepts that previously could only be expressed in two-dimensional pictographs, gestures or through dance, developed into more complete ideas.

As our communities grew larger and larger, the leaders became more than just the best hunters. They earned a responsibility to the community: to keep members safe from danger, safe from other communities, and safe from each other, to some extent. And they had to make decisions that were in essence planning for the future.

To keep people safe from each other, they had to make rules that protected the community. Some of these rules were probably carry-overs from our simpler beginnings, such as the practice of driving away undesirables. If you couldn't help the community, you would probably be removed from the community. The words we used for sickness and deformity, for example, were probably close cousins to the word we used for death. The former often brought the latter.

Rule Number 3: Don't Spoil It for the Rest of Us.

In those early times we categorized things, we needed explanations for why things happened, and we understood the concept of cause and effect. We broke this down into noticing a pattern, forming a question, and giving an explanation.

The Pattern: Every day, the sun rises in the East and sets in the West.

The Question: Why does the sun rise and set every day?

The Explanation: Someone carrying a burning stick is running across the sky.

Before we had language, we knew the sun rose and set, and we may have even marveled at it, especially when it was accompanied by magnificently colored clouds or it was larger and richer than normal. Then language allowed us to place the question and express the answer. And at first the answers were pretty simple, like the example above. But as anyone with a child knows, the answer to a simple question is always followed by the more difficult question: Why?

This had our leaders in a pickle, because though they made the rules and had the basic answers, they were typically all brawn and no imagination. They didn't know why things happened any more than the rest of us. So they turned to the tribe members who had imagination, who could give a more complete explanation to why things happened. And our first priests were appointed.

They were called wise men, or shaman, or seers, and they served a valuable purpose in the community. It goes without saying that the people with the best imaginations were probably good at figuring out problems and remembering patterns like which berries made you sick and which berries kept you regular, so this **combination lead them to** become the healers in the community as well as the storytellers. Thus our communities gained another layer that contained someone who wasn't as important as a leader, but was more important than the common follower.

More vital though, was our need to know what causes and effects governed our superstitions. It boiled down to two things: Benefits and Detriments. In our minds, some things we did caused benefits. For example, rubbing the spear with the bear fur made the spear better in our minds, made us brave, improved our hunting skills, and kept us well fed. Conversely, rubbing the spear with the musk sack from a skunk forewarned our prey we were on the hunt, made us poor providers, and drove our gatherer-wives into the arms of hunters who knew how to use a spear. That was a detriment.

The holy men of the community defined most of the benefits and detriments relating to superstitions. They watched for patterns, remembered what worked and what didn't work, and crafted the explanations. If you think this is far-fetched, contemplate this: as late as the 1500s man thought asparagus grew from discarded ram's horns, and women as late as the 19th century believed they could get pregnant from touching something a pregnant woman touched, like a doorknob.

Through the imaginations of the holy men, communities learned what made the sun, moon and stars move across the sky. They learned what caused the wind and where lightning came from. But that ever-present question from childhood still plagued the leaders and the holy men. And when Joe the Stout was struck by lightning and died, the people asked, "Why?"

A quick thinking holy man answered, "Because he pissed off the spirits of the sky."

And religion was born.

Our need for cause-and-effect explanations was satisfied, even if we couldn't remember what exactly Joe the Stout might have done to anger the spirits. What was important was that people could comprehend the idea of retribution. To anger something as abstract as the rain clouds was dangerous for more than just Joe the Stout. What if the spirits of the sky decided to punish the whole community with floods or drought for Joe's indiscretions? That was a great place for the leaders and the holy men to start manipulating the mindset of their followers. "Don't spoil it for the rest of us. If you do, we'll punish you to keep the spirits happy, we'll drive you out of the community or worse, we'll kill you for being a troublemaker."

This type of explanation probably carried the leaders and holy men through hundreds or thousands of similar events, until someone everyone knew and loved, Old Gray-Haired Sally, was struck by lightning. Then they asked, "Why was Sally killed? She never did anything to anger the spirits." Once again, that quick-thinking holy man stepped forward and said, "True. But she didn't show the spirits the proper respect."

We all learn in our childhood how to respect something that's dangerous. We learn how to respect fire so that we don't burn down the house, how to respect a dog we don't know by giving it plenty of space, and how to respect our mean old next door neighbor by staying out of his yard and not climbing his fence. In ancient times, showing respect for something that was more powerful than you was an easy concept to grasp.

So the people asked the holy man how they should show the spirits respect and prevent deadly lightning strikes. He thought on it a while and devised a plan. "Give the spirits something they want," he said. But what would a spirit who lives in the dark rain clouds want? The holy man was stumped. His imagination couldn't leap past his own needs and wants, so he told them what they would understand, too. "Give them food." The next and obvious question was how to **get the food up to them. Some people probably threw food at the** sky. Others walked to the top of a mountain during a thunderstorm and threw food at the clouds, most likely getting them electrocuted. The holy man made a recommendation. "Toss some food into the campfire, so that it will travel into the sky on the smoke."

And sacrifice was born.

With sacrifice comes the peace of mind that someone else is looking out for you. Hunters sacrificed to the spirits of the hunt. Fishermen sacrificed to the spirits of the rivers, lakes, and seas. Gatherers sacrificed to the spirits of agriculture. Women who wanted to have children gave to the spirits of fertility, and women who were already pregnant, did likewise to have a healthy child. They showed their respect, gave the spirits their dues, and imagined nothing bad happening.

Well, bad things still happened, but people had the piece of mind that the bad things didn't happen because they had disrespected any spirits. Looking at it this way, it sounds a lot like extortion. Here are the spirits, ethereal Mafioso's, demanding protection payment from a frightened and helpless population. "Give us food on the trails of smoke or we'll visit unpleasant humors on you!"

At least it was job security. Soon holy men were educating people from every walk of life, every type of craftsman, hunter, and leader, telling them how and where and when to make sacrifices to ensure that the spirits would be benefactors, instead of enemies.

Genesis 4:3 In the course of time Cain brought some of the fruits of the soil as an offering to the LORD. ⁴ But Abel brought fat portions from some of the firstborn of his flock. The LORD looked with favor on Abel and his offering, but for Cain and his offering, he had no regard.

Simple sacrifices evolved into more complex ceremonies. At the beginning of particularly nasty seasons, like winter and the monsoon months, the sacrifices were magnified in the hopes that the spirits that dominated that season would have mercy on them and lessen their plight.

The spirits were eventually given names and they each had personalities, depending on the community. On one side of the mountain, where the sun shined and temperatures were moderate, the spirit of the mountain was a benevolent being. On the shady side of the mountain where it was always cold and the people were plagued with avalanches and mudslides, the mountain spirit was considered a nasty fellow who had it in for everybody.

Holy men found that their answers to the people's questions often had to make the people feel good, instead of always having to carry the weight of the world on their backs. Sometimes they wanted to know that there were rewards in life. Simple rewards, sure, but rewards nonetheless. And the ultimate nagging question everybody asked was, "what happens when we die?"

Some would say that the dead get to live with the spirits. Probably whichever spirits they made sacrifices to in life. Some holy men would say that you didn't go anywhere when you died. You got to hang around the village, watch your grandchildren grow up, and occasionally party with everybody on certain nights of the year.

There was one honest-but-foolish holy man who said, "Nothing happens when you die. There is no afterlife and your body becomes worm food." He soon found himself with a bloody mess on his hands. In a society without consequences, people did whatever they wanted because they didn't understand the concept of greater good, self-judgment, and good for goodness sake.

Rule Number 4: Maintain the Status Quo

The spirits were happy with their smoke and food, but other leaders and holy men were noticing the problem the foolish holy man experienced: lawlessness. They didn't know what laws were, but **they knew they needed them.** "Play nice," "Respect each other," and "Do what I say or I'll bash your head in," wasn't good enough when your nation was made up of thousands of people making sacrifices to thousands of spirits. New holy men cropped up out of nowhere, and self-appointed leaders instigated revolt at the drop of a hat (or lion-skin robe). So they had to figure out a way to keep people from screwing up the status quo.

The leaders and the holy men recognized the mistake the foolish shaman made. So they devised a plan to frighten the masses into respecting each other. When they were asked, "What happens when we die?" they responded coldly, "We are judged."

"Judged? Judged for what?" the masses wanted to know.

The holy men were serious. "We are judged for all the things we do during our lives."

"All the things we do?"

"Yep."

"And then what? What happens after we're judged?"

"Well, if you were a good follower, something good happens when you die."

"And if we do bad things? If we're bad followers?"

"Then, uh, something bad happens."

This conversation probably took place during hundreds of thousands of ceremonies across hundreds of years. It was the same philosophical dialogue between people who wanted to live like animals and the leaders and holy men who wanted to mold us into a functioning society and keep themselves in control.

The argument for posthumous judgment was an easy one to make, since we were already preprogrammed to need and understand cause-and-effect relationships, and being superstitious, it was easy to convince us that we were surrounded by spirits who watched our every move and kept tabs on the deeds we did. The more difficult argument was what the end result of the judgment would be for each of us. Different holy men came up with different afterlives.

There aren't enough pages in this book to describe all of the possible prehistoric explanations for an afterlife. Suffice to say that the hunter-gatherer societies were fearful of the dark and the unexplained, and understood the cause-and-effect rules that governed their superstitious lives. Without much imagination, they probably applied a lot of during-life aspects to the afterlife. For the typical primitive hunter-gatherer, a positive afterlife was full of sunlight, had lots of animals to hunt and berries to gather, and was devoid of anything that wanted to eat him. A negative afterlife was dark and barren, with nothing to eat and lots of hungry predators.

Consider these precursors to our modern concepts of an afterlife. They're pretty advanced for what I think prehistoric man envisioned, but they make my point:

Greek afterlife

One belief, often attributed to the Greeks, was that everyone languished in the afterlife, and that the degree to which you languished was directly related to your judgment score. Your deeds, your social standing, and your successes were the basis for your judgment. A poor score meant you would languish more. A good score, say you did lots of good deeds in your life and you were a patron of the arts, meant that the afterlife was probably just more of a bore than a whole lot of languishing. Basically, you got to stand on one side of the river on dry land and watch people on the other side languish in the swamps and be devoured over and over again by various nasty creatures. This belief wasn't much of a motivator for the common Greek man.

Norse afterlife

Another belief that I remember from a 6th-grade primer on Norse mythology was that the afterlife was a big party, with lots of ale drinking and fighting. The "good" people in the village (those who died in battle or being brave) got to party all night long, hack each other apart with no lasting injury, and sleep all day. The "bad" people in the village (the cowards) had to serve the drinks all night long, and clean the urine, vomit, and body parts off the floor all day. Not too far off from a modern day college fraternity, except that it lasted more than four years. The Norse also believed that people who died of illness or old age had to spend eternity in a nasty, cold, foggy, barren place called Niflheim, which was ruled by the goddess, Hel. That was a great motivator for getting out there and dying in battle.

Another thing I remember from that book was that the Norse god of thunder and war, Thor, had a hammer named Mjolnir that was crafted by two dwarves. The dwarves belonged to a blacksmith union that didn't require them to read design specifications, which resulted in the finished product having two defects: its handle was too short and it was too heavy to pick up. They devised a work-around for the first defect by adding a strap so it could be swung without grasping the handle. They devised a work-around for the second defect by crafting Thor a pair of iron gloves and a belt that doubled his strength, instead of just fixing the damn hammer.

(Early) Hebrew afterlife

The spirit world for ancient Jews didn't actually exist until after the final judgement. Until then you were just dead. But after judgement day, the spirit world was an insubstantial existence in darkness. Those who were "good and faithful" Jews in life spent eternity near the light, which was God, and those who were failures at performing the duties of the faithful, i.e. worshipping God without question and following the Ten Commandments, were doomed to wander in the cold darkness without the warm comfort of the light. They would have to stand outside the window of God's house and gnash their teeth.

Sound familiar? Ancient people were afraid of the dark, afraid of the cold, and afraid of starvation. What worse punishment could befall you? They believed that whether you were in heaven or hell was defined by how close you got to be to God.

The 4 commandments

So we have the four main rules for the primitive tribe that were designed to keep everybody alive and helped form the tribal unit into a functioning society. Break one of these rules and you would definitely be punished, if not by the leader, then by your fellow tribe members:

>   Be Quiet
>
>   Do What the Leader Says
>
>   Don't Spoil It for the Rest of Us
>
>   Maintain the Status Quo

Those rules lasted a long time; probably thousands of years. But they needed to be broadened when the leaders got tired of getting complaints from followers that someone's favorite lucky spear was being used by another hunter, someone's lucky berry basket was being used to catch fish, or someone's favorite mate was being seduced by another tribe member with a bigger tent and a bigger fertility talisman.

That brings us to the basic rules for modern man, in modern society, with modern issues, defined by leaders concerned for the well being of their community, and holy men concerned for the continued existence of their place in society.

The Ten Commandments

So the story goes that while they were wandering in the desert after escaping the Egyptians, Moses brought the Israelites to Mt. Sinai to receive the Law from God. He warned the people and their leaders not to follow him up the slopes because "the power of the Holy Spirit would kill them," wink wink, then headed up the mountain with his faithful-but-rarely-remembered assistant, Joshua. According to Hollywood legend, Joshua was a stone-carver, so I think he was probably the one who wrote the commandments.

I like to imagine Moses and Joshua sitting on the mountainside try-ing to make rules for a new society and really just talking about the things they hate, like when Moses' brother, Aaron, steals Moses' magic staff to do parlor tricks at weddings, or when people try to sleep with their wives, or how much it irks them when their teen-age kids don't show them any respect. They worked out their issues and the top ten action items became the rules they would bring back down to the people.

The conversation took a long time, because like any brainstorming session it was easy to get off track, plus Joshua was taking notes using hammer and chisel, which was still pretty slow, even if he dropped the vowels and used that cool new Egyptian short hand he learned in Heliopolis before the plagues.

Here's the thing that bugs me about the Ten Commandments. Moses climbs the mountain to get the tablets from God, but it takes 40 days for God to deliver ten simple rules. That seems kind of long for a guy who only took six days to create the entire universe. If I had hired Him to do some repairs on my house based on His earlier work history, I would have been outraged by the outcome.

Me:	So, Yahweh. I hear You built the entire universe.
Yahweh:	Si, señor Phelps.
Me:	And they say You did it on a shoestring budget with almost no materials?
Yahweh:	Si, very little to work with.
Me:	I've got this little project. It's a bathroom renovation that shouldn't take more than a week. Would You be interested in the job?

Yahweh: Si. It would make me very happy to do it.

Me: Great! Can You start Monday?

Yahweh: Por supuesto. I'll bring my son, Jesus along to help. He's a very good carpenter. See you Monday.

[40 Days Later...]

Me: Yahweh, what's the deal? It's taken you almost two months to do a job you could have finished in the blink of an eye!

Yahweh: I'm sorry, señor Phelps, but my skill with the tile, it's not so good.

Me: Well, don't expect me to pay for all this extra time...

Will I get death threats for that one? I hope not. How about some homework, instead?

Homework

Quick, grab a pen or pencil and, without consulting your trusty Bible or the Internet, write down the Ten Commandments in the following box, or as many as you can remember. Make sure you put them in their proper order:

1. _____
   _____
2. _____
   _____
3. _____
   _____
4. _____
   _____
5. _____
   _____
6. _____
   _____
7. _____
   _____
8. _____
   _____
9. _____
   _____
10. _____
   _____

Now, look them up on the Internet and read about the variations. Different Christian denominations have different versions of the ten you take for granted; the Jews have the "10 Utterances" or "10 Words" or "10 Judgments" which some believe are merely subject headings for 613 commandments in the Torah; while in the Koran,

Muslims have an entirely different take on them, considering the Judeo-Christian commandments a corruption of the original rules.

In case you don't have access to the Internet, a Bible handy, or a preacher living in the room your parents rent out, I've included a copy of this famous list at the end of this chapter.

So, I think religion started with the fear of lions, then was added to by wise men explaining nature's processes, and finally refined by tribal leaders maintaining the order of the society under their dominion.

Its primary purpose was to keep the calm, productive, single-minded masses from becoming the wild, unproductive, lawless masses. Just read William Golding's "Lord of the Flies". Ultimately, the rules of religion and the fear of an afterlife of eternal punishment have kept us in line for a little over three thousand years.

How was religion organized?

You might argue that by quoting from the Bible for my examples, I'm mixing a lot of modern man, which is to say Biblical man, with my description of the religious life of prehistoric man. Tough titty said the kitty when the milk wouldn't flow.

My ignorance of history and anthropology doesn't mean that it didn't happen the way I describe it. Consider the following examples I've illustrated. I imagine that they are the basic structure for authority and religion in Stone Age society.

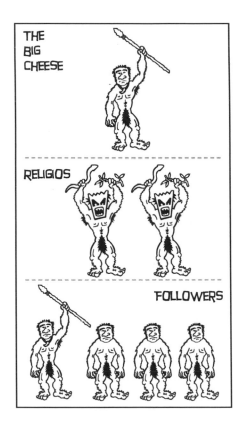

Example 1: The Big Cheese.

A chieftain who has claimed his leadership through brute strength but defines his ascension as divine right rules the tribe. His word is law, both socially and spiritually. Beneath him are loyal holy men who educate the people and enforce his rules. When another brute-strength leader takes over and claims his place at the top of the chart, the holy men bow to his superiority.

You're familiar with this idea. It evolved into the kingdoms you know in history like Europe's monarchies, the Roman Empire, ancient Egypt, etc. When a new king is crowned, the religious leaders are there to proclaim that the ruler's ascension is ordained by heaven and that one of the king's jobs is to protect the church, temple, or whatever local religious institute needs protecting.

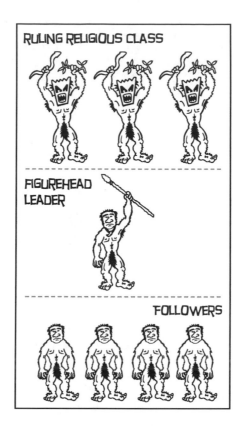

Example 2: Ruling Religious Class

A council of holy men rules the tribe. They lay down the law and have the final word in anointing the leader. Meanwhile the leader is essentially the head of security for the society, often deferring to the holy council for all administrative decisions. This is commonly called a theocracy. But in the Stone Age I think the leaders would have to be extra superstitious or complete weenies to let the holy men take over.

You see this today in countries where the strength of the local religion and the faith of the followers is mightier than the ability of the military class to subdue them. Often, the military is populatetd by faithful religious followers, which lends an extra layer of authority to the religious class.

Example 3: The $3.99 Combo Deal

A committee of brute-strength leaders and holy men rules society. There are only two layers to this society, where committee members share equal authority, and less gets done without a clear definition of responsibility. This often leads to disagreement and division that opens the door for one of the previous societal structures to take form, where either one brute-force leader takes charge, or where a theocratic council becomes the ruling body of government.

Another model is missing from this illustration. It's where you have one supreme religious leader who presides over a council of holy men, with followers beneath. That's the same as the first example, because the leader claims his position by divine right, using brute strength to rule, or the strength of his faithful followers and the power of fear to keep the masses in line.

There are more variations, but in my opinion these are the easiest to pull over on the common followers. The basic premise is effortless to invent, simple enough to understand, and easy to enforce. Plus, it was easy for me to illustrate with my three doodles of cavemen.

These structures are fluid. A nation of people is likely to migrate through all three models during their history. Even bouncing back and forth between the different types until they settle into one they really like, or until some other country decides to impose their belief system upon them. And we've seen it occur through most ancient cultures, and even most modern ones.

The Big 10

From my Revised Standard Version of the King James Bible (1952, paraphrased), here are the Ten Commandments:

1. You shall have no other gods before me.

2. You shall not make a graven image for the purpose of praying to them.

3. You shall not take the Lord's name in vain.

4. Remember the sabbath day and keep it holy.

5. Honor your father and your mother.

6. You shall not kill.

7. You shall not commit adultery.

8. You shall not steal.

9. You shall not bear false witness against your neighbor.

10. **You shall not** covet your neighbor's house, wife, manservant, maidservant, ox, ass, or anything else that your neighbor owns.

Much like The Lawgiver on the planet of the apes, Moses gave the first Jews the ten *fundamental* rules for all the laws we hold near and dear in The United States. That is why the Religious Right in America are called *fundamentalists*.

Doodle Time: Can you draw a burning bush?

Remember: it grows on the side of a mountain, it talks, so include a mouth and make it saying something, and don't forget the berries. The best bushes have berries.

Bringing it up in conversation

Chapter 2

They say a well mannered person should avoid three topics in conversation with co-workers or at dinner parties: sex, politics, and religion. But I think religion is a perfect ice breaker. Start innocently by asking what people think of the Catholic church protecting pedophiles. Ask how far up the hierarchy the blame should climb. Does it stay in the diocese and stop at the pedophile's bishop? Arch-bishop? Cardinal? Ultimately you'll be asking if the Pope is an accessory to the sexual molestation of innocent children and protecting known pedophiles. Then move on to more interesting topics like God sanctioning slavery, murder, and the seduction and rape of virgins. (Read Exodus 21-22).

If people invented religion, then can gods be "born?"

Yes.

Every god is born from our imagination, from the way they look at their spheres of influence, to their nation of choice and name. What was Yahweh's name before it was YHVH or Jehovah? The way I read it, God called himself El Shaddai, El the Mighty. You could interpret it as God Almighty, too. But since the Canaanites worshiped a god named El, doesn't it make sense that the Jews and the Canaanites worshiped the same god at some point in their history?

Exodus 6:2-3 And God said to Moses, "I am the Lord. I appeared to Abraham, to Isaac, and to Jacob, as El Shaddai, but by my name the Lord I did not make myself known to them."

Does this mean that the patriarchs (Abraham, Isaac, and Jacob) worshiped a different god than Moses, or only that he went by a different name? That would be an odd thing for a god to do. I think they worshiped different gods. As the nomadic people moved around the Middle East and Northern Africa, or were enslaved by various conquering nations, they adopted lots of different religions, until they made their beliefs more permanent by writing things down.

Every religion starts out small and grows as new followers join the ranks. Some religions get exterminated by others, some join others to become a new one, and some just fade away from lack of use, like the stationary bike in my bedroom that has slowly disappeared beneath a pile of clothes waiting to be folded.

> Some religions get exterminated by others... and some just fade away from lack of use.

Does God have a body?

Most religions depict their gods as physical beings at some time or another. They might eventually say He is everywhere and everything and unseen or invisible, but when you get down to it, God walked with Adam in the garden of Eden. You can't get much more physical than that, unless they wrestled in the garden. Plus, if He didn't have a physical shape, how could anyone "sit on His right hand side"? Or how could He have made man in His own image?

Throughout history, people have seen God as a physical being, rather than an abstract concept. They might picture him as a larger than normal human who sits on a gigantic throne, or as an old man with a long white beard, or as a four-armed man with an elephant's head. In every case, the image is drawn out of that person's imagination, or for those without imagination, the image is borrowed from something they are familiar with in nature, or drawn from somebody else's imagination. Ganesha, the Hindu god with the elephant's head is called "the mover of obstacles." He gets things out of your way for you. Well, what have Indians used for thousands of years to move things like fallen trees, groups of people, and building materials? Elephants. So, it stands to reason that their God with the power to move obstacles would have an elephant's head.

Test yourself. Everybody has their own mental image of God in their mind. What does your God look like? Write it down here and then ask some friends what their God looks like without telling them what you wrote. Compare theirs to yours afterward.

_____

_____

_____

_____

_____

Having trouble? Here are some specific questions you can answer to help you work out the details.

Is He young or old?   _____

Is He a specific race?   _____

Does He have ☐ hair, ☐ a beard, or is He ☐ bald?

Does He wear clothes like:

☐ a robe ☐ angelic armor ☐ a sweater ☐ other _____

Is God a She instead of a He?   _____

Is She hot?   _____

Is God regular human-sized or giant?   _____

Does God have any animal characteristics like:

☐ horns ☐ goat legs ☐ wings ☐ other   _____

Now, try your hand at drawing what your God looks like.[1] If He stands on clouds or rides a giant turtle, feel free to add them.

You're not going to believe the stuff I saw last night

Some people actually see God, some hear Him, while some see Him and hear Him. Some see angels or get visited by the Virgin Mary. In the old days, the biblical times, those people were called prophets. Today we call them whackos, nut jobs, psychos, or schizophrenics, even though there are still people—quite a few people—who believe in visitations, messianic visions, and will pay a fortune teller hundreds of dollars to tell them that love is just around the corner or that their dearly departed husband is resting peacefully in heaven,

---

1   If you want to share your artwork with the author, go to www.toenailsbook.com for instructions on how to send it.

waiting for her to join him.

Adam walked and talked with God in the Garden of Eden. Moses conversed with a burning bush. Mohammed heard His voice in a cave. Joan of Arc was given explicit orders from God to defeat the English. (God loves France more than He loves England.) And many messiahs, messengers, and televangelists claim to be direct conduits of God's message.

Were the prophets (from Ishmael and Ezekiel to Mohammed) really talking to God, were they making things up? Could it be that they were actually crazy? If they were crazy, how did they convince so many people to believe in their visions? It's simple if you have ever talked to someone who is delusional. They so completely believe what they are saying that you start believing it, too.

There is persuasion in self-confidence. Sometimes when I talk to homeless people or read conspiracy theory web pages, I find myself getting dangerously close to believing what's being said. It isn't hard when the person seems to be making a good argument.

Even in our lifetimes we've seen new religions born out of someone's imagination. New Age gurus, a reincarnated leader from Atlantis, aliens, self-proclaimed psychics, and hypnotists who take advantage of people. Some would argue that they have been around as long as the mainstream religions, but only recently have they coalesced into the formal, well-defined organizations that they are today. Lawyers help with that.

Some people think astrology is a religion and some don't. Some mainstream religions used to incorporate astrology into their belief system, or still do. Some people think it's a science and others think it's a joke. Personally I think it takes responsibility, control and blame away from us for our actions. "Oh, you know, he's a Capricorn, he couldn't help but run over that monkey."

There are new "buffet" religions, where followers pick and chose what they want to believe from other religions. The origins of these various bits lend validity to the religion as a whole. Like people who believe in heaven, God, and angels, but don't think you have to follow the rules laid out in the scriptures to get into heaven. "Be good, love your neighbor, and God will accept you into paradise with open arms." I know some people who adamantly disagree with that philosophy. Then there are famous rock stars who think they can call themselves Esther and claim to be high priestess of some mystic branch of the Jewish faith after they were raised Catholic and spent decades living a Godless life.

I have a problem with people who believe in religions that are obviously made up, almost as much as my problem with literalists. Take the Church of Latter Day Saints (Mormons), for example. There's no doubt that the religion was invented by a guy in 1830, and yet it has swelled like a boil to over twelve million followers around the world, is considered one of the fastest growing religions, and has even been granted acceptance among some of the other Christian denominations. Some would argue that Mormons are "good" people, with excellent work ethics, tight family bonds, healthy morals, and a strong community. But that doesn't let them off the hook for believing something that a con artist named Joseph Smith invented 170 years ago.

Sure, I said that people can believe what they want as long as they don't force those beliefs on other people. But isn't that what missionaries do, force their religions on other people? That's one of the main tenants of the LDS church, to spread the word.

How about a religion where they believe that 75 million years ago a galactic ruler named Xenu enslaved mankind's spirits in a volcano and blew it up with atomic bombs, forcing their souls to be trapped in mortal bodies? Don't laugh. It's considered a real religion, popular among movie stars, but I won't mention its name because it has the most aggressive legal team known to man and I don't want to lose the proceeds from the sale of this book to a religious organization.

If it doesn't hurt anybody, what's wrong with believing in a religion that was made up a few generations ago? It isn't any different in my opinion than believing in a religion that was made up two thousand years ago. I don't know why it rubs me the wrong way, it just does.

I can't guess how many religions over the last three or four thousand years started but failed to take hold. Or, they started but were absorbed by another religion before they became entrenched, worldwide. At the same time Christianity was being developed and gaining a foothold, there was a religion called Mithraism that was gaining popularity in the same regions (Rome, Greece, Turkey, Southern Europe, etc.). Not a lot is known about it, but some historians believe that early Christians borrowed several aspects from it, for example eating the flesh of the resurrected hero (Mithras) to gain everlasting life. Or maybe both religions struggled for popularity during the first couple centuries of their existence, and after Christianity won the contest it gained the use of all the icons, symbolism and holy places throughout the kingdoms where both were worshipped.

What is the formula for a successful religion? Confucius and Buddha knew it. So did the folks who invented Vishnu and Jehovah. Jesus Christ and Mohammed were men with great recipes for successful spin-off religions that won blue ribbons at the religious masses county fair. Most recently, Joseph Smith figured out the formula when he invented the Latter Day Saints and L. Ron Hubbard constructed a religion—in our lifetime—that is gaining a high-profile following and legitimacy, at least among celebrities.

I often ask myself what it would take to start a mainstream religion. **I used to joke with friends that we should invent** one just to earn a little extra gambling money for our trips to Las Vegas. That is until this morning, when I came up with one in the shower.

I wonder what it would take to erase all religion. As entrenched as faith and superstition is in society, I think God would have to come down from heaven Himself and tell everyone He doesn't exist in order for them to stop worshipping Him.

I dreamed I was God

I dreamed that I stood upon a hill that overlooked a flat and featureless world and that God appeared around me and within me and the voice of God spoke through my voice. The voice of the Creator, Ahura Mazda, Yahweh, Allah, God, flowed from me so that the whole world could hear and understand.

All the dieties, prophets and teachers throughout history surrounded the hill and stood as individual angels beneath me and around me. They looked up at me as I spoke and then turned to the world and smiled with the love of understanding.

Beyond the ring of angels, all the people of the world stood around the hill and could see all the angels and understood all of their voices. When I spoke, the people and angels nodded their understanding and when the angels spoke, the people understood them, too. The spirit of their words as well as the words themselves were understood.

God's hands were on my shoulders and His voice rang from my mouth, saying, "let there be no classes of people."

Then, from among the angels, Shiva, Brahma, and Vishnu stepped forward and addressed all their worshipers and the rest of the world, saying, "there are no classes. No one is bound by a caste system. Men and women are equal" Then they embraced and became one angel, stepping back into the ring of angels.

God's light showed bright around me and His voice rang from my mouth, saying, "you are not bound by rules for enlightenment."

Then, from among the ring of angels, the ten gurus, the teachers of the Sikh, the Gurmat, came forward and threw open the door and it broke into a thousand pieces that became birds and flew away. They stopped reciting their hymns to say, "The path is not through dress nor appearance, nor self sacrifice of worldly goods, nor repeating prayers and hymns. There is no path, for you are living life and your enlightenment is your awareness of those around you." Then the Gurmat embraced, became one angel, and stepped back into the ring of angels.

From my mouth God's voice spoke to the world, "there are no chosen people."

Then, from among the ring of angels, Moses stepped forward. He lifted the Law and it shattered into a thousand birds that flew away. God's name was erased from his head as if a heavy weight was lifted from his shoulders and he smiled at his people. All the covenants of God faded into dust.

Then, from among the ring of angels, Mohammed the Prophet stepped forward and stood beside Moses. The five pillars rose from the Earth around him. He held the heavenly, golden copy of the Koran aloft and its pages tore loose and became a thousand birds that flew away. The five pillars collapsed into dust, and he smiled at his people.

Then, from among the ring of angels, Abraham stepped forward and put one hand on Moses and the other on Mohammed. "You are my children," he said, "and with everyone else we are all the children of the world." In unison, Moses and Mohammed said, "there are no rules for food. Neither in what can be eaten, nor in the preparation. Be healthy." And then Abraham embraced Moses and Mohammed and they became one angel. They stepped back into the ring of angels as the light of understanding and compassion shined in the eyes of their people.

God lifted me into the air and his voice, which was my voice, said, "The Word is not the way." He set me upon the hilltop, with both feet firmly on the ground.

Then, from among the ring of angels, Jesus Christ stepped forward and addressed all the world. "You are one with everyone else," he said. "The way is not through me, nor in believing in me, but in caring for others. There is no path to redemption, for you have redemption without me and without prayers. It is in your actions. I will not return, and there will be no messiah, no end days, no Armageddon. There will be no final judgement." The Holy Spirit left him like a cloud, became a thousand birds and flew away. Jesus stepped back into the ring of angels.

God became my voice and His light and His presence was gone except for the sound of His voice through my voice.

Then, from among the ring of angels, Siddhartha Gautama, the Buddha, stepped forward and said, "life is not suffering. Life is the opportunity to end the suffering of others through compassion and understanding." The light of the universe faded from his head and he stepped back into the ring of angels.

And I said from the hilltop to the whole world, "we are equal."

Everyone in the ring of angels, the teachers, prophets, gods, saints, gurus, and ancestors looked at me and their divine mantles faded.

Their lights were extinguished and their burdens were lifted. They smiled as they embraced each other and became a single, ordinary person. The ordinary person walked into the crowd of all humanity and became one with the rest of the world.

And I said to the whole world, "care for one another."

All of the holy places of the present and throughout history, the churches, temples, mosques, shrines, grottos, rocks, cathedrals, walls, ponds and such, considered touched by God, the prophets, the angels, the saints, creation, and all things divine, became ordinary places devoted to feeding the hungry, learning about the nature of the universe, and healing the sick. Their magic faded. They were appreciated for their beauty and place in history, but they were no longer held sacred, exclusive or unapproachable.

And I said from the hilltop to the whole world, "heal the sick, feed the hungry, comfort the downtrodden, and understand those who are different."

It started to rain on the hill. And God's voice from me said that there was no need to pray anymore. It said that the world would raise its voice for us, so that all the people of the world could use their voices to share their love among each other and to learn from each other.

The vedas of the Hindi became the sound of rain and stopped being recited altogether. The sallahs of the Muslims became the sound of rain and stopped being sung and spoken. The Jewish prayers, the Amidah, the Shema Yisrael and all the others, became the sound of rain and stopped being repeated. The prayers, and hymns and liturgies of the Christians became the sound of rain and stopped being spoken and sung. All the other prayers of the world became the sound of rain and wind and waves and rivers.

And all the people stopped praying. They listened to the beautiful sound of the rain and the wind and the waves, then started talking to each other for understanding and compassion.

Then I closed my mouth so that God's voice did not issue forth, and God spoke three secrets to me, that were not to be shared during the dream, but would be taught in the waking world.

Then the hill flattened so that I was as one with all the people surrounding it and held no station above them, and so that no person would hold a station of authority above any other person. And God's voice rose out of me an hovered above everyone.

"I will leave the world to you, now," God said. "I will become nothing, as all the religions, creeds, patriarchs, divinities and misunderstandings have become. You are alone and there is nothing and no one to come. Love each other and yourselves. Share. Do not subjugate or oppress others. When you die, you end, and only your worldly actions are left as a reminder of what you were and what you did."

All the people of the world understood the voice. We embraced each other and communicated with each other, and felt compassion. We knew we were one family from now on.

"This is the end of all religion," God's voice said. "I will not change my mind or send another prophet, teacher or messiah. There is no heaven, so there will be no news from me or any others ever again. Remember what I told you, for I will not be back with anything else."

I and all the people of the world understood. We smiled and held each other as the peace filled us.

And then God was gone. And I woke up.

And that's how easy it is to start a new religion. I wonder how many people will ask me what those three things were that God whispered to me.

How does it get so big so fast?

Why doesn't anyone believe in Paul Bunyan anymore? Did they ever? Somebody did, a long time ago. I know I did when I was growing up. It made perfect sense. Paul, his big blue ox named Babe, and all the fantastic things they did. You know, of course, that Paul Bunyan and Babe created the Grand Canyon by dragging Paul's axe like a plow. There's proof, too. It's called, "The Grand Canyon."

So, some drunken French Canadian rebel lumberjacks in 1873 turn one of their own into a demigod with campfire tales about the size of his feats, then the lumber industry in the 20th century used sanitized versions of the myths as a public relations tool, and voilà a kid in second grade actually believes an ox can grow to be bigger than a zeppelin and be as blue as the sky. In fact, generations of kids believed in Paul Bunyan, or used to, the way they believe in Santa Claus and the Easter Bunny. It seems to me that religion or at least the stories within the religious framework are no different. David and Goliath, Cain and Abel, Samson and Delilah, are all the same as Paul Bunyan and Babe, except that at no point in the telling of the stories does somebody say, "You realize, of course, Jimmy, that these stories are just made up, right?"

If a myth as wild as Paul Bunyan grew from stories about a real man, could the same be said for King David, Noah, Saint George or Jesus? I think it is entirely possible. Somewhere during the retelling, most stories get some exaggeration, even if only a little for dramatic effect. It's in our nature to turn the story of a mundane event into a tale of miraculous adventure.

What about miracles?

Why don't miracles happen anymore? Not sad faces appearing on tortillas or statues weeping, I mean real miracles, like lasting peace descending on the Middle East during Rosh Hashanah or a 747 crashing into a crowded football stadium and nobody getting hurt (not even the drunken pilot). I had a ten inch plastic statue of Sid Caeser that wept. It was in my family room and cried every year during "sweeps week." Damn those network executives who plan what I get to watch during prime time.

The Bible is full of miracles. But since I think men wrote the Bible and added exaggerations wherever they wanted, I believe biblical miracles are just plain stories that have been embellished with each retelling, from Noah and his ark, to Jesus Christ and his loaves and fish. In order to keep somebody's attention you have to exaggerate the details. Plus it's like the telephone game, where you whisper something in someone's ear and they try to repeat what you said to the next person. By the time it's gone around the classroom, it's totally different from how it began. I think you can pick up bits of truth in religious manuscripts by reading between the lines, or just by using your imagination.

Did Jesus perform all the miracles attributed to him in the New Testament, or did the guys writing the letters exaggerate the facts? Was it "five thousand men, not counting women and children," like Mark describes, or was it "a large crowd," the way John describes it? How many are in a crowd? Could it have been five?

If in actuality, the story was about Jesus feeding eighteen men with five loaves of bread and two fish (Jesus, the twelve Apostles, and the five guys who followed them up the mountain), would the story have been as compelling? What if later editors of the texts went back and changed "five" to "five thousand?" That's a better story, huh?

I think Jesus was pretty savvy when it came to convincing people they could get by with less. And he was big on using metaphor.

Maybe there were five thousand people waiting for food that day and all He had was enough for five plus his disciples, so he gave everybody a pinch of bread and waved a fish over their heads. Then He said to the crowd, "Verily, if you were starving in the desert, then this would have been like a feast before you and you would be satisfied. Go, and be hungry no more."

Who can argue with that? People went home happy. Plus, he and his disciples still had the fish left over at the end.

Do we join religions to be part of a tribe?

I think that's a big part of it. We're tribal creatures. The way that dogs prefer packs and deer prefer herds, we like to be part of a community.

It starts with the family unit, which is the fundamental tribe that we naturally group ourselves into, grandparents, parents, and children. Add siblings to the mix, and the families of the spouses and you have a tribe. We need it to survive as a species, since our children are too helpless to be left alone in the wilderness.

The family unit expands into groups of family units, villages, communities, regions, and nations. Until recently, the size of our tribe was at the mercy of geographic boundaries and the resistance or encroachment of other tribes. Historically, we identified ourselves and our tribes by various commonalities, such as color, language, clothing, ethnicity, ceremony, locale, and other social or cultural markers.

As we mix our tribes more on a global level, we find other ways to identify ourselves as members of distinct tribes. Whether it's as a cowboy, punk rocker, blue-collar worker, yuppie, Christian, Sikh, Navaho, blonde, tattooed person, snowboarder, or any other way you can think of to tell yourself apart from others or to draw others similar to you into your group. For example, I drive a pickup truck, and consider myself a pickup truck driver. I don't consider myself a

truck driver, though, as that implies a whole different class of people. I like the make and model that I have, but I don't put stickers on
the back window that shows me peeing on another brand of pickup
truck. Some folks do and I think that's taking the tribal thing a little
too far. Dodge trucks peeing on Chevy trucks peeing on Ford trucks.
I think that's silly.

Then why do the Redwings suck?

I primarily grew up in Texas in the 1970s and '80s, where although
we had lots of different types of sports, the only one that mattered
was football. I had heard of lacrosse, soccer, and hockey, but had
never seen a game played.

When I moved to Colorado, I began noticing a curious thing. Lots of
people had bumper stickers on their cars, trucks and SUVs that read,
"Redwings Suck." It didn't say anything else, so I was completely
in the dark. Who were these Redwings? Are they dangerous? How
have they offended the people of Colorado in so visceral a fashion
as to warrant a bumper sticker expressing their hatred? I was clue-
less, until I asked a co-worker.

It turns out that in a 1996 professional hockey game, a Colorado
Avalanche player nearly crippled a Detroit Redwings player in re-
taliation for an injury inflicted upon his teammate in a prior week's
game. After that, the two teams developed a rivalry that spurred a
series of historic and bloody fights over the years. The rivalry is so
strong that many of the fans even hate each other.

Why would someone want to drive around with a sign on his back
that says, "I hate the thing you love?" Whether it's a sports team,
the make of truck they drive, whether or not they like cowgirls, hate
their ex-husband, support the President, or believe Jesus Christ is

represented by the outline of a chrome fish, they want other people to know where they stand. They might do this to feel loved and a part of something. Or they might do this to make other people question their beliefs. Or they might do it because "it's cool." Either way, they have defined their tribe with a bumper sticker, t-shirt, tattoo, necklace, hat, hairstyle or voting record.

That's tribal.

Is it hard to invent a religion?

Nah. It's easy. I invented one this morning. I haven't named it. I'll leave that honor to the historians and theologians that follow.

My religion is centered around the god BoGo the Devourer™. He is the god of rabid consumption. He travels through the universe, carried on the back of his holy cash cow, buying everything he can get one of his four hands on, and consuming it.

His appetite is endless. His taste has no boundaries. His magic credit card, though maxed out, always has room for one more unnecessary purchase.

Most American's are rabid consumers, and are thus BoGoists like me. I call them Unknowing BoGoists. The ranks of my religion are swollen with fat and fatuous Americans and they don't even know it. Whether it's full price or in a bargain basement closeout sale, BoGo the Devourer™ wants it, needs it, and could care less about it.

BoGo the Devourer's mantra is "Buy it now! Buy it all now! Then buy something else!"

BoGo the Devourer™

Here's a little fact you may not know. BoGo the Devourer's holy sceptre is also a back scratcher and a candy cane.

You don't have to be a con artist like Joseph Smith, a bandit like Mohammed (may his name be praised), or a deluded farmer like Abraham to start a religion. Just make up an avatar (*don't forget to trademark and copyright it*), construct a simple mythology around it, and watch the money come rolling in.

DOODLE TIME: What is BoGo the Devouror™ devouring? Fill his hands with the sacred articles of consumption.

Hint: perhaps he's spinning a basketball, taking a photo with his new digital camera, balancing a tray of lemondrop martinis, and holding aloft his favorite crescent wrench? Or is it a gallon of gas, a freshly grilled hamburger, a portable TV, and a bouquet of flowers? You decide. Don't forget that he sits atop a pyramid of credit cards and/or is transported on the back of a holy cash cow.

The devil made you do it

Chapter 3

Beware of the people who try to convince you that you have the Devil or a demon in you making you believe that you're an Atheist. There are no devils and demons, except those who sell religion through paid programming on TV.

We are responsible for the bad things we do. We're responsible for every lie we tell, every extra slice of pizza we eat when we're on a diet, and every racial joke we tell when our "racial" friends aren't around. There is no external diabolical force that makes you do things you don't want to do. You're either giving in to your own desires, like being greedy, selfish and lustful, or you have a hormonal imbalance or chemical dependency in your brain that you can't control.

In this chapter I'll explain why I wrote this book in the first place. It's actually a pretty funny story.

I'm not a theologian. I have no credentials, no education on the subject of religion other than my exposure to it over the years. This is only a collection of opinions and observations.

Most of my opinions are in reference to Western religions since my experience with religion has been primarily "Christian" in nature. (Some might venture to say "Judeo-Christian.") And some might say that the majority of unethical, fanatic, intolerant Christians I have been exposed to growing up were the hard-core Southern Baptists from my hometown in Texas. I call them Bible-thumpers. They're fanatics. Most of the religious people I know call themselves Christians, though many Christians argue over what that means.

I know a few people who are Jewish and I have watched the movie, "The Ten Commandments" a lot over the years. I have a few Buddhist friends. I know a couple people who practice Hinduism. And I know a handful of New Agers and pluralists who like to mix bits of various religions together to get a nice creamy paste that smells good and helps soothe dry hands. Overall, I don't know much about what they believe specifically.

I'm a devout Atheist.

There, I've said it, and there was no lightning from heaven, nor fire and brimstone.

I don't have much more to say about it and I wish it wasn't such a big deal, but I often find people asking me, "How can someone as smart as you not believe in God?" I usually furrow my brow at them and respond, "Ya know what? I never asked myself that. Gee whiz, since I'm a smart feller, then thar must be a Gawd." That kind of sarcasm typically doesn't go over too well, and so the yelling begins.

The original title of this book was:

Houston I

(The First Book of Houston)

(or, A Letter to the Houstonians)

Mid 1990's, a friend of mine in Houston, Texas, went through a transformation. In the course of a week, he went from being a non-practicing, not-sure-about-the-nature-of-things C&E Christian (Christmas and Easter) to a Bible-thumping, twice-a-week-calling-to-witness, zealous, "you're going to burn in Hell, and the Jews killed Jesus," fall-on-the-floor-babbling evangelical Christian.

Actually, he wasn't that bad. It just felt that way because we talked almost every week for ten years without mentioning God or Jesus, other than to say, "God, it's hot this summer," or "Jesus, can you believe the stuff the President is getting away with in the Oval Office?"

Then, without warning his weekly phone calls changed. He used to call to ask me if I watched the latest Dallas Cowboys game, or to ask me if it's okay to cheat on his wife (I usually said, "no," depending on which question he asked). I'm not much of a football fan. But one day in 1997, his calls became more proselytizing in nature, with lots of, "Jesus is my personal savior," this, and, "I'm blessed with God's love," that. Plus he started talking about things in the Bible *as if they actually happened.* It got tiresome pretty quickly, seeing as how I've been an Atheist over twenty years.

Most Atheists find Atheism in college when they take their first philosophy class. Then, after they graduate, they land a job, get married, and find God again when they witness the birth of their first child. I think it has something to do with seeing the placenta[1]. Luckily, I've never seen one close up; otherwise I might not be writing this book. Please don't mail me one.

I, on the other hand, became an Atheist in high school. I've been an Atheist ever since my rude introduction to the cruel reality of male erectile dysfunction and how quickly a teenage girl will tell her friends about it. It was a one time event, I assure you (or I assure myself), but it opened my eyes to the dark, heartless oblivion of the universe.

I'm joking. There was no relation between me becoming an Atheist in high school and my first experience with "failure to perform." The real joke is that it hasn't been a one-time event. But I'm learning to live with the occasional blow to my ego.

This writing project really started with the poisoning of a dog. That's true, I'm not joking. At one end of the universe a dog gets poisoned in Houston, Texas, and at the other end of the universe you find yourself reading this book. Kind of creepy, huh?

Here's the story:

---

1   \Pla*cen'ta\, n.; 1. (Anat.) The vascular appendage which connects the fetus with the parent, and is cast off in parturition with the afterbirth. Source: Webster's Revised Unabridged Dictionary, © 1996, 1998 MICRA, Inc.

That friend of mine—the one I mentioned who used to call me about mundane, everyday things like picking up girls at the office where he worked, or asking me if he should cheat on his wife, who turned around one day when he "found" Jesus and started witnessing to me—lived outside of Houston on a parcel of land, with dogs, cats, horses and such. Well, he called me one day to tell me that he had irrefutable evidence of the existence of God, and that if I listened to him I would see and understand the gloriousness of his revelation. He had a story to tell me about God answering his prayers.

My friend's name is Danny and I've known him since fourth grade. I'm going to editorialize a little during the retelling to share my opinions of his thought processes along the way.

It seems that though Danny lives in the country, his house sits relatively close to the property line, putting him very close to his neighbor's house. Danny has never been very friendly with his neighbor, probably because Danny has a penchant for relieving himself off the back porch after he's had a few beers. It's Texas, after all, and in the spirit of the late, great Lyndon Banes Johnson and the later, greater John Wayne, he always felt it was his God-given right and patriotic duty to pee off his porch. Occasionally he would wave to his neighbors while doing so.

Well, the not-so-friendly neighbor had a dog that was never very nice to Danny, either. It was a barker, the kind of dog that would bark all night just to hear its own voice. Out in the country, past the oil refineries of Sweetwater, there's not much you can do about that. Crickets chirp, katydids buzz, bullfrogs croak, and dogs bark. It's the tantalizing symphony of the Texas twilight. It didn't help that the dog spent the nights in a small chain-link confinement referred to as a "run," that was spitting distance from Danny's bedroom window. Barking, barking, barking.

The dog barked at everything. It barked at the wind. It barked at Danny when he was peeing off his back porch. It barked at every pickup truck that drove down the street. It barked at the neighbor cats that tormented it with their fancy acts of fence balancing.

And one night, after a twelve-pack and a late night of watching the History Channel, the barking was just too annoying to Danny. He was tired and he had to wake up early the next morning for work. So what's a guy to do? Well, just before the crack of dawn, after a sleepless night, Danny walks to his workshop, takes some poison, rolls it in a slice of bologna, and feeds it to the neighbor dog.

I was mortified

I couldn't believe I was hearing this. Despite the fact that I was at work, in a room with four co-workers who eavesdropped regularly on my phone conversations with Danny because they knew an out-landish tale was being told. I couldn't believe that my long-time, childhood friend—a "best" friend—would be telling me this. And I couldn't begin to guess how his story would give me irrefutable evidence of God's existence.

Needless to say, the poisoning shut the dog up. No more barking, and Danny was able to get an hour of shuteye before he had to get up and go to work. Which he did.

During his commute to the office, Danny started feeling a tug of remorse. Well, actually I call it remorse. He called it nervousness. He worried that while he was at work the dog would die; the neighbors, suspecting foul play, would have an autopsy performed; and he would go to jail for killing the dog. The nervousness grew, and he started to pray to God that he didn't get sent to jail.

As his anxiety mounted, he changed his tactics and started praying for God to save the dog. By noon, after several hours of praying, worrying, and not getting much work done, Danny decided to run home during his lunch hour and check on the dog. As he left town and drove through the countryside, he prayed some more, adding a prayer that he not be caught in the act of disposing of evidence, should the need arise.

To his surprise and relief, when he arrived at home and checked the neighbor's dog run, the little rascal was alive and (seemingly) well, in its enclosure. Sure enough, the poisoned bologna was in the cage with him, having been vomited up sometime in the morning.

Danny retrieved the poisoned meat product and threw it in the trash. He gave the dog a pat on the head, breathed a sigh of relief, thanked God for the inter-vention, and promptly called me when he got back to his office to share the news of the miracle.

I was speechless, incredulous, incensed, fuming, and disgusted. Dumbfounded, the most I could summon was to ask if he was go-ing to take the dog to the vet to make sure it was going to be okay. "Why?" he asked, since God had already saved the dog. I couldn't believe my ears.

Danny was surprised that I didn't see the miracle in this story. He had fed the dog poison, prayed to God to save the dog, and his prayers were answered. It was a miracle! It was as plain as the nose on my face.

I explained to him that most animals tend to vomit when they're fed poisoned meat. It's a natural response. If they vomit before the poison gets into their bloodstream or before it does any permanent damage to their organs, they survive. It's not a miracle, it's the way nature works. It's how we survive in the wild when we don't know what's good to eat and what's not.

Let's not go into the fact that he had committed a crime, which I told him. I was bound to inform the authorities, which I told him. He had become less of a man, less of a human, and had dashed every shred of respect that I had for him, which I told him. He thought about it, and then came to a conclusion. And I thought I couldn't be more surprised or disgusted.

He said the Devil did it.

I was wrong thinking I couldn't be more surprised. On the phone with me is a grown man—the father of several children, a husband, and a businessman—rationalizing that he wasn't responsible for his actions. He was placing the blame on a supernatural being, saying it entered his sleep-deprived body, took over just long enough to poison one of God's creatures, then exited, leaving him the victim.

Did I mention I was disgusted and appalled?

Then he told me he would pray some more to make sure he had gotten all of the Devil out of him. I told him he needed to spend some time in jail and that he needed to get some professional counseling.

Well, his plan to open my eyes to the wonders of heaven didn't work. I couldn't talk to him for weeks, and when he would call to witness to me, I told him I was too busy and too angry with him to talk rationally. I half-heartedly tried to convince him to talk to some other Christians, maybe some broader-minded Christians, to see if maybe he was on the right track. Obviously, whatever he was learning in his church didn't seem quite right to me and I wanted him to get some other viewpoints to make sure he was hearing the same message.

He wouldn't give up the fight, though, to save my heathen soul. He continued to call and witness, leaving messages about the latest miracles he had seen. For example, he was late for work, prayed not to get stuck in traffic, and miraculously had a lot of green lights on his commute. It was a miracle. God was answering his prayers. More proof that He existed. I think Danny was confusing coincidence with divine intervention.

In the weeks following that horrifying phone call, I received voice-mails from him explaining how he feared he would have to spend eternity in heaven watching me burn in hell. He was good at repeating what his preacher told him in the Sunday sermon. And I felt sorry for him in more ways than one.

Finally I told him that I am and always will be an Atheist. I know it. I'm positive of it. He couldn't convince me otherwise. And I would gladly write a letter about it so he could read it and understand my point of view. So he took me up on it. "Write me a letter about it," he said, "and prove to me that there's no God."

Well, it started as a letter to Danny, but has grown into this collection. Like I said, at one end of the universe a dog gets poisoned and at the other end of the universe you find yourself reading this book.

Allow me to stress one point: I will not prove that God does not exist. That was Danny talking, not me. I'm only writing my opinion about religion and my own Atheism. It's not a scientific treatise on whether or not divine matter exists. Please don't mail me any. It's a simple explanation of my beliefs.

Let's start with my original statement: I am an Atheist.

Webster's Revised Unabridged Dictionary, © 1996, 1998 MICRA, Inc. defines the word Atheist this way:

```
\A"the*ist\, n. 1. One who disbelieves or denies
the existence of a God, or supreme intelligent
Being.
```

Pretty simple. Note that it doesn't say, "One who writes a book to disprove the existence of a God, or supreme intelligent Being." I do not believe God exists, thus I am an Atheist. I don't have to prove God doesn't exist.

Some might say that I'm a secular humanist. I don't really know what that means and I haven't spent much time comparing secular humanism to Atheism. I just know that I don't believe in God.

So there you have it. Now you know what prompted me to write this book. To be totally honest, if all Danny had become was a devout, practicing Christian who occasionally witnessed to me, I wouldn't have had a problem with his rebirth, conversion, brainwashing, or whatever you want to call it. A big motivator for me was that he had become a literalist. He literally believed what was written in the Bible, and he literally believed that when he did something wrong, it was the Devil doing it. And he believed that in the afterlife I would actually be burning in hell, cooked alive in the lake of fire for all eternity.

To Danny, there is no symbolism in the Bible, just historical fact, and a divine truth. The universe was created in six days a few thousand years ago, Jesus is the begotten son of God, Lot's wife was turned into a pillar of salt, and there had never been rain until Noah finished building his boat.

I, on the other hand, believe that the world has existed for billions of years, that all creatures are descended from simpler forms, and that the almost infinitely large universe is not built solely to house human beings until the moment when God decides to call home the faithful and hold a "day of reckoning."

The story of the great flood is
a perfect example of literalists
accepting a myth as a true story.

DOODLE TIME: Draw animals marching 2-by-2 into the ark.

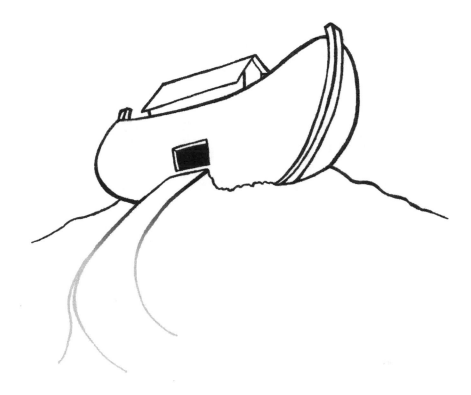

Extra credit for unicorns, bigfoot and dinosaurs.

Be a pro at arguing your point

Chapter 4

You don't have to be an expert on religion to have an opinion about it, and you don't have to be a theologian to argue over the usefulness or validity of organized religion. Just read a little about it. Pro or con, do a little research on your own beyond simply listening to the preacher (brainwashing) telling you what to think.

There are lots of books on the subject. That's why libraries and book stores have entire sections devoted to it. If you want insight into the religion you believe, read about it from a historical perspective. For example, learn about ancient Jewish history from the perspective of those nations that conquered them. By seeing that the Babylonians and Egyptians had pre-existing Great Flood tales of their own, you can surmise that the story of Noah's Ark was incorporated by the Jews into their own mythology from those conquerors.

...Then why do I have nipples?

As I mentioned before, the title of this book was going to be called, Houston I (The First Book of Houston) or, A Letter to the Houstonians. But I began to think that one of the reasons I'm an Atheist, aside from a failed highschool fling, is that I see proof every day that we weren't literally plastered together from clay and dirt by some magical sculptor's hands, but instead evolved from more primitive life forms. I'm reminded of this every time I trim my toenails, which sadly, according to my wife, isn't often enough.

Since I could only think of one explanation why I have toenails, and no explanation why I have nipples, I decided to call this book, "...Then why do I have nipples?" completing the larger sentence, "If God molded man from clay, then why do I have nipples?" But the photo on the front cover of my bare chest disturbed the test market bookstores, so I fell back on the alternative, and went with my toenails. Also, I had to think of the women readers who might ask the question on the cover, with the answer being too obvious, and I would alienate half of my potential book-buying audience.

So, I ask you, why do I have toenails? I don't use them, other than to pass the time when I need something to dig under or trim. I can't dig in the dirt with them or turn the head of a screw. I occasionally use my thumbnail to turn the head of a screw, if the screw is really

Charles Darwin asked himself why men have nipples, too.

loose. But I can't put the torque on and tighten a screw down very well with my thumbnail and I can't use my toenails for that at all, even if it was a life or death screw-turning mission.

My wife is convinced that I have toenails solely to torture her when we sleep. But I say they're not long and sharp, it's just the angle at which they grow that makes them feel long and sharp when they brush against her leg in the middle of the night.

The one explanation for having toenails I could think of is that if my calf itches, I use the toenails of the opposite foot, usually the big toe, to scratch it. Could it have been in God's plan to give me toenails just so I could scratch the back of my calf? Why would we have such a redundant tool? I can reach down with my fingernails and scratch my calf if it itches. And we already know (from the thumbnail and the screw) that fingernails are much better tools than toenails. And why have four extra toenails on each foot if we only need the big one?

Could it be that toenails are proof that we are descended from some other animal, a creature that used its feet to climb trees, dig in the dirt, and defend itself? And if they are proof of such evolutionary beginnings, does that mean we weren't crafted from clay? And would that mean the Bible is inaccurate?

Does it matter?

I guess the larger question is, does it matter if the Bible is inaccurate? Some say that the message is more important than the historical fact. They might also say that the events described in the Bible are meant for discussion as metaphors, to teach us important lessons, the way parables teach us. For example, you can learn a lot from the fairy tale about the boy who cried wolf. It doesn't mean that there was ever really a boy guarding the farm or a wolf terrorizing him.

The same goes for the stories of Noah, Moses, and Jesus. Some of them make sense and offer us advice on how to live in a righteous way. Most of the stories are a bunch of bologna written thousands of years ago to give a displaced people some national pride and later to be used as the foundation for a new cult. I don't think that's heresy. It's just a statement of fact.

I say, yes, it matters if the Bible is inaccurate. This is to people who say that the Bible is "divinely inspired and infallible," which means that those who wrote the books, or compiled the letters, or translated the information, or decided which books stay in and which come out, were guided to do so directly by God and that His hand does not waver on the steering wheel. I agree, to the extent that if God had written the Bible, it would be a flawless and perfect document.

But, if the Bible had a flaw, or if it contradicted itself, which is a type of flaw, then that would be proof that it wasn't divinely inspired and that it was in fact written, compiled, translated, edited, and redacted by men. And to be more specific, it was written by men with an agenda. They were inspired to tell these stories and construct this religion, but it wasn't divine inspiration.

How many contradictions or flaws does it take before a religious document is obviously just the work of men? Sounds like the beginning of a bad joke.

Matthew 27:5 - So Judas threw the money into the temple and left. Then he went away and hanged himself.

Acts 1:18 - With the reward he got for his wickedness, Judas bought a field; there he fell headlong, his body burst open and all his intestines spilled out.

Some scholars argue that Matthew, the person who wrote the simpler description, was addressing a Jewish audience and was just making a point: Judas killed himself; while Luke, who supposedly wrote the second description, was addressing a Gentile audience and needed the extra gory details to capture their attention. I like the second description because it has pretty gory details. Maybe Luke was an ancestor of George A. Romero[1].

My interpretation: these two guys wrote about a third guy they knew or heard about who killed himself. Since they didn't actually see him commit suicide, they relied on second-hand accounts or they used their imaginations to describe his end. The fact that they wrote these accounts decades after it may have happened didn't help them with their accuracy.

That contradiction is a simple example of a couple guys writing their letters, probably a little loopy from wine, incense, dancing girls, old age and moldy bread. Plus it was the age of the New Testament, modern times. Writers were prone to make mistakes, even those who were divinely inspired, since they had new fancy quills, easy flowing inks, and parchment. And, what of the writers of the Old Testament? They were a serious lot who had to deal with the divine inspiration of a pretty rough and tumble, sometimes-vengeful God, so they had to be extra careful. They had a thick, stiff parchment that

---

1   George A. Romero: Hollywood writer/director of such great gory films as *Night of the Living Dead, Dawn of the Dead, Day of the Dead*, and the 1974 documentary *O.J. Simpson: Juice on the Loose.*

tended to roll-up while they were writing if their scribe assistants weren't paying attention to hold it down, and they had the tricky job of writing from right to left with a twig. Plus, before they started writing their stories on paper, they carved them into wooden sticks, a pretty labor-intensive process considering the lengthy genealogies they liked to go on and on about, which was probably why they dropped the vowels. And before that, they passed the stories down verbally. Imagine how happy they were to get curly papyrus and a blunt stick to write with instead of all that oral memorization. Still, it wasn't an easy task.

Malachi 3:6 - "I the Lord do not change."

Numbers 23:19 - God is not a man, that he should lie, nor a son of man, that he should change his mind.

Exodus 32:14 - Then the LORD relented[2] and did not bring on his people the disaster he had threatened.

Sure, the book of Malachi was written by, that's right, a guy named Malachi, who was a minor prophet that didn't do much more than write one book. Meanwhile, Exodus was written by Moses, perhaps the most important character in the Old Testament, who performed all kinds of cool magic tricks with his staff. Which of them was right? Is the Lord permanent and unchangeable, like Malachi says, or did He change His mind at Moses' insistence? I don't think divine inspiration would show favoritism, whether you are only known for writing one book in your lifetime, or whether you are credited as the liberator of an entire nation of people.

This contradiction example doesn't mean the events in the Bible didn't occur, and they don't tell us that the Bible isn't true. They tell us that regular people wrote what's there, not God.

Belief in Him may have inspired it, but He didn't divinely guide the writers. Thus, the Bible is flawed and not literally true. So the people

---

2   The King James Version (in English) quotes (Ex. 32:14), "And the LORD *repented* of the evil which he thought to do unto his people."

who think that all the world's myriad of languages came from God's affront over a tower being built in Babel are wrong.

Here's another side thought: were the characters in the Bible manipulating the stories as they played out? There was exaggeration and borrowing myths from other cultures, for sure, but what about flat out lies to make themselves look more important than they were?

Is the following story, from Mark, chapter 11, a triumphal entry into Jerusalem or grand larceny?

[1]As they approached Jerusalem and came to Bethphage on the Mount of Olives, Jesus sent two disciples, [2]saying to them, "Go to the village ahead of you, and at once you will find a donkey tied there, with her colt by her. Untie them and bring them to me. [3]If anyone says anything to you, tell him that the Lord needs them, and he will send them right away."

[4]This took place to fulfill what was spoken through the prophet:

[5]"Say to the Daughter of Zion, 'See, your king comes to you, gentle and riding on a donkey, on a colt, the foal of a donkey.'"

[6]The disciples went and did as Jesus had instructed them. [7]They brought the donkey and the colt, placed their cloaks on them, and Jesus sat on them. [8]A very large crowd spread their cloaks on the road, while others cut branches from the trees and spread them on the road. [9]The crowds that went ahead of him and those that followed shouted,

"Hosanna to the Son of David!"

"Blessed is he who comes in the name of the Lord!"

"Hosanna in the highest!"

[10]When Jesus entered Jerusalem, the whole city was stirred and asked, "Who is this?"

[11]The crowds answered, "This is Jesus, the prophet from Nazareth in Galilee."

It's one of my favorites. This quote is an example of the true nature of Jesus' gang as they wandered the countryside, "spreading the word." It strikes me that in the first paragraph Jesus instructed two of his disciples to steal two donkeys. (In some translations, I think they only steal the colt.)

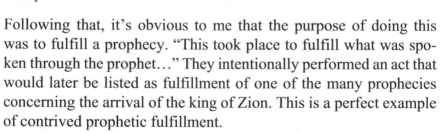

This is an account of an event. It is not a parable. It is not a portion of a larger story that the meaning of which would be taken out of context when read independent of the whole story. It's a simple fact: Jesus told his disciples to steal two donkeys (a mother and her colt). Regardless that they were supposed to tell anyone who asked that they would be returned, Jesus still ordered his disciples to break the 8th commandment.

Following that, it's obvious to me that the purpose of doing this was to fulfill a prophecy. "This took place to fulfill what was spoken through the prophet…" They intentionally performed an act that would later be listed as fulfillment of one of the many prophecies concerning the arrival of the king of Zion. This is a perfect example of contrived prophetic fulfillment.

In my opinion, one example of faking the fulfillment of prophecy counters all the other examples of prophecies being fulfilled.

What about faith?

Believing in something that you cannot prove is faith at its simplest. I know people who say they can't prove the existence of God, but they know He exists. Their evidence is in the sunrise, every child's laughter, puppies, rainbows, an act of kindness, and every case of childhood leukemia that goes into remission. The beauty of a flower garden is proof enough that God is smiling down on them. And above all else, how could there be love without God? Love is this invisible, undeniable emotion that has no explanation. It's solid proof that God exists.

I feel exactly the same way. I have no proof that God does not exist, and yet I feel it is absolutely true. My proof of God's nonexistence is in every man's nipples, in the survival instincts of every living thing, in every case of childhood leukemia, and in every epidemic that ever killed thousands as it swept from thatched hut to thatched hut. And this feeling of attachment, ownership, responsibility, and intertwined existence that we call love is no more proof than poetry is proof of God.

The euphoria of love, whether it is a chemical reaction or something more, is a force that helps us propagate our species. What is the greatest form of love? A single Red Sox fan would say it's his love for his team. A couple would tell you that it is the love two people have for each other, until they have children. Then they would say the greatest form of love is the love a parent has for its child. This makes perfect sense in nature: love of self (self preservation); love of spouse (need to reproduce); and love of offspring (to guaranty the continuation of your DNA). I don't think love is just social science and chemistry. There is much more to it than that. But I can't explain it any better. I don't think it flows down on us from Jesus in heaven or someone else like ice cream on a warm day dripping down the side of the cone.

I like love. In fact, I love it. It feels good. It makes me happy, when it's not causing me chest pains, and gives me a little boost when I'm feeling down. That's the boost of knowing someone out there loves me, whether that someone is my wife, my mommy, my senator, or the rock band I saw last weekend whose poster is hanging on my bedroom wall. (They understand me.)

We all need that and I pity those people in the world who haven't experienced love, or aren't loved by someone, somewhere.

...Then who the heck is Saul?

The Apostle Paul wrote half of the New Testament. Many Christians don't know who Paul is, and how significant he is to their religion. They think he was one of the disciples who walked around with Jesus. But he wasn't. In fact, he never even met Jesus. But, without him Christianity would have remained an insignificant spin-off slave cult among the Jews.

Allow me to introduce you to a fellow who lived near the Mediterranean about two thousand years ago. His name was Saul, he claimed to be a Roman citizen, he admittedly liked cracking Christian heads, and he got his just desserts in the end.

You know him as Paul. Or, you know him as Paul who was Saul of Tarsus. The story goes that he was a Pharisee, the roughest kind of Jew in those times. The Pharisees were the equivalent of today's "bad guy" pro wrestlers. And Saul was the worst. He was clever, ruthless, and as I said, he liked to crack skulls.

In a nutshell, the Pharisees sent Saul to Damascus to beat up on the Christians there who were busy converting good Jews away from the orthodoxy. On the trip, and perhaps while he was transporting a wagon full of Christians to certain skull cracking, Saul was blinded by a bright light, had a vision of Jesus, and was converted to Christianity. Some might add that the conversion took place while he was on vacation in Arabia, recovering from his blinding vision.

I like to find modern explanations for miraculous events. Call me crazy, but when I think of the great flood, I wonder if in the original story (if there actually was a flood) it was just a sizeable river valley that flooded, instead of the entire planet. And I further wonder if Noah was an average farmer who threw a couple goats and chickens into his fishing boat when the river crested its banks and flooded his farm. Could that have been the story? Over the years, obviously, it outgrew itself until it became a metaphor for God's wrath. Who wants to hear the same old story about thrifty old Noah who saved his goats and a chicken named Shemp, when they could hear the story about a crazy man who built a giant zoo-ship on faith alone, at God's demand, gathered two of every animal on the planet, and turned his back on all of the pitiful drowning people who made fun of him while he was working so hard? Me, that's who. And probably lots and lots of young Hebrew children for the ten centuries that story was told around the campfire.

Another example of explaining ancient accounts in modern terms would be the blinding of Saul, his vision, and his conversion on the road to Damascus.

Let me walk you through my account of Saul's story. Here's a relatively young, tough-as-nails, assertive rabbi-in-training, faced with a daunting task: get the Christians to stop spreading the concept that Jews do not have to follow all of the old school rules. He finds himself near Damascus with a problem. No matter how many skulls he cracks, they just keep turning the other cheek!

He had quotas that he wasn't meeting; probably a two-thousand head-cracked milestone by the end of the first quarter, with high percentages of positive transition back to Orthodox Judaism, or else he wasn't going to get his Passover bonus. He was bummed about this and wondered how he would explain to his mother that he wasn't going to be able to take her to spend the summer visiting her sister in Cicilia because he couldn't complete his project.

He's on the road to Damascus, looking forward to his chance to stay in one of the most technologically advanced cities in the world. One of his Pharisee coworkers had recommended a great place to get hummus, and a nice inn to stay in while he was there. Suddenly, he falls to the road, blinded and has a vision.

What would cause a young, healthy man to collapse and see a light so bright that it blinded him? I've thought about it and decided on the following three most probable scenarios:

1. **He had a migraine.** A real nasty one. The type of migraine where all you want to do is crawl into a dark corner and drive a spike into your head. Symptons: loss of bodily control (collapse), seeing bright lights and/or being blinded by a bright light, and pain-induced delusion (vision).

2. **He had a stroke.** Mild enough that he recovered and was able to continue traveling, write lots of letters (at least thirteen), and duke it out with the founding fathers of the Christian church (the original apostles). Symptoms: collapse (it was a stroke, after all), seeing a blinding white light, and experiencing a degree of delusion or confusion during the episode.

3. **He was hit by a rock.** A young Christian with a bandaged skull decided it was payback time for Mr. Saul and brained him with a rock. Rock slinging was a common practice in those days, seeing as how they had so many just lying around, and surely Saul had provoked enough people with the skull cracking he so enjoyed, for one of them to return the favor.

There could be dozens of reasons why he fell down, was blinded, and had a vision, but I tend to accept my third explanation as the closest to truth, mainly for the poetic justice, but also because at the time it was a struggle to be a Christian. Everybody except the poor and downtrodden persecuted them, and just when they started to make some headway in what is now the capital of Syria, word comes from Jerusalem that a major skull-cracker is on his way to enforce the will of the Pharisees. **People are nervous because they know he's** coming, and they want to stop him. So a kid from the West Bank (of the Barada River) breaks the rule about being nonviolent and plays David and Goliath with Saul's noggin.

As I envision it, the kid is immediately full of remorse, and he drags Saul's unconscious body to his house, in the hopes that his mother can nurse Saul back to health. The boy prays Saul will recover so he can ask for forgiveness.

Saul was a smart guy. He wanted to get inside the heads of his enemy, noodle around a bit, and find out why they so stubbornly clung to their convictions. And during his convalescence in the house of his attacker, he had the opportunity to learn first-hand what the Christians were all about. I believe that in the process he realized what a cash cow this new religion could be, especially for an entrepreneurial individual like himself.

Of course, this is a more nefarious explanation for Saul's conversion than the thought of him actually being blinded by God's grace, seeing divine visions, and finding himself believing that Jesus was the Son of God, who died on the cross for Saul's sins and was resurrected. It's easier to believe that Saul was actually converted to the cause, through the selfless kindness of the mother of the boy who nearly killed him. Besides, those Syrian girls are really cute.

Though I like to give people the benefit of the doubt, I prefer to be a cynic about Saul.

I think Saul considered himself a visionary. He had a vision after all, and saw where Christianity was going. It had started as a branch cult within the Jewish community, but he could tell that people of all walks of life, except the ultra-orthodox, would like the message about the kingdom within the here and now, love thy neighbor, and the golden rule.

It was going to be a good racket for anyone in a position of power who could get in on the ground floor. And he was just the man for the job. But first he had to convince the other apostles that his plan had merit.

That was a little bit of a struggle, but after lots of arguing, yelling, and forceful persuasion, he got his way. Remember, he was a lot younger than the original, surviving apostles who actually walked around the desert with Jesus, and he had a lot more energy. He wore down the ones that were still alive, and convinced them to broaden the message so that it applied to the Gentiles[3].

And he wrote lots of letters. Most of the letters were probably to investors, describing a business plan for a worldwide enterprise that would rake in more money over time than could be stored in hundreds of Solomon's temples, and would command nations and drive political policy throughout half the world for thousands of years. The other letters were some outlines for the basis of the religion, with parables he had heard about Jesus, plus some exaggerations of a few of the miracles the Christians believed Jesus had performed.

And since he was a smart, shrewd businessman with a flare for the theatric, he convinced a lot of people that this new, crazy religion was good for most everybody. In those days most people were poor peasant class without hope of ever achieving anything in this life, so the concept of being given the kingdom of heaven was quite tempting.

Christianity as we know it comes primarily from the New Testament of the Bible. For some denominations, that's the four gospels, Acts, the thirteen epistles of Paul, the seven general epistles, and Revelation, according to my King James Version of the Bible. That's twenty-seven letters, almost half of which were written by the Skull-Cracker of Tarsus.

I wonder what the New Testament would have been like if that Christian boy had never thrown that rock at Saul on his journey to Damascus, if he had never been nursed back to life by a cute Syrian Christian, and if he had never realized the business opportunity his vision presented. Would Christianity exist at all? Or would it be something we wouldn't recognize today? A lot of modern Christians think that they have returned to a form of Christianity that was more like what it was during the time of the Apostles, or just afterward.

There are some Christian sects that discount the writings of Paul

---

3   Basically, anybody who wasn't Jewish.

Books of the New Testament:	Generally accepted as the Author:
Matthew	Matthew
Mark	Mark
Luke	Luke
John	John "The disciple who Jesus Loved"
Acts	Luke
Romans	**Paul**
1 Corinthians	**Paul**
2 Corinthians	**Paul**
Galations	**Paul**
Ephesians	**Paul**
Philippians	**Paul**
Colossians	**Paul**
1 Thessalonians	**Paul**
2 Thessalonians	**Paul**
1 Timothy	**Paul**
2 Timothy	**Paul**
Titus	**Paul**
Philemon	**Paul**
Hebrews	Anonymous (Maybe **Paul**)
James	James (Jesus' brother)
1 Peter	Peter
2 Peter	Peter (or Anonymous)
1 John	A different John (the Apostle)
2 John	John the Apostle
3 John	John the Apostle
Jude	Jude (Brother of James)
Revelation	John "the Divine" (a different John with a vision)

entirely, and model their beliefs purely on the writings of the people who actually knew Jesus, but they're few and far between and are scoffed at by those who believe in Saul's conversion. Plus, many thousands of them (especially in Egypt and the Middle East) were hunted down and exterminated by Roman Christians.

Honestly, I don't think Saul had the foresight to see where Christianity was headed. Who could have known in the first century that a little more than two hundred years later the Roman Empire would adopt it as the official religion, effectively making it the single most peaceful religion in the West backed by the strongest army on the planet?

Plus, I think there's more to Saul's story than we talk about in Sunday school. Namely, he was from Tarsus, which is now Turkey. I wouldn't put it past the Jews of biblical times (or anybody of biblical times) to discriminate against people from other places, especially Turks. Jews from Israel and Judah probably looked down their noses at Jews from other countries, even if they were card-carrying members of the All Skull-cracking Pharisee Society (ASPS). Saul claimed to be a Roman citizen. This may or not have been true, but it was a great way to travel, and a great way for a rough-and-tumble Jewish kid to keep from being tossed into jail every time the police came across him in a back alley cracking Christian skulls.

A CENTURIAN steps into the dark alley and lifts his torch. He sees SAUL holding a nearly catatonic, battered young CHRISTIAN MAN by the collar of his blood-soaked robe.

Centurian: What's going on here? What's all the commotion?

Saul: Nothing, officer.

Centurian: Whole lot of blood for 'nothing.'

Saul: It's really nothing, officer, I'm just reminding this Jew boy where he comes from.

Centurian: Jew? He looks like one of those fish-drawing, blood-drinking Christians...

Saul: Yeah, that's just what we're trying to straighten out. He doesn't want to participate in the celebration of lights this year, and I'm trying to change his mind.

```
Centurian:      By punching him in the head?

Saul:           More or less.

Centurian:      It's making a lot of noise. Worrying
                the neighbors.

Saul:           I'm sorry, officer. We'll try to keep
                it down.

Centurian:      Maybe you should just break it up,
                before I run you in.

Saul:           But officer, I'm a citizen of the
                state.

Centurian:      A Roman citizen?

Saul:           Yes. I'm here on business from
                Tarsus.

Centurian:      Oh. Well that's different then.
                Carry on, citizen, and have a nice
                evening.
```

```
The Centurian walks off with a wave. Saul returns to
thrashing the Christian Man.
```

I think Saul was a sad, lonely individual. He was torn between a homeland he didn't want, an empire that didn't trust him, and a religion that didn't accept him wholeheartedly because of both.

His only option was to become part of something completely different. An opportunity was handed him in the form of a fresh new religion that he could muscle-in on and help define, with the help of some of the other religious beliefs of his day.

Not too shabby for a kid from Tarsus

Saul went from being the insignificant strong-arm of a fast-becoming obsolete, close-minded, ultra-exclusive religious group, to being the primary architect of an all-inclusive, evolving, open-to-interpretation cult with aspirations of becoming a full-fledged world-wide religion. In the process he got a new name, he got to spread The Word without people running from him, and he achieved sainthood.

His Jewish mother probably never forgave him for dashing her dreams of him becoming the first rabbi in their family. She also stopped inviting him to temple after he married that shiksa from Venice named Irene. Nonetheless, she can be proud of him now for all the great things he accomplished, like writing thirteen or fourteen letters.

If the founder of a religion is a certifiable crackpot, does that make the religion any less valid? For example, would you follow a science fiction writer or a con man to the ends of the Earth and give him or her all your money?

DOODLE TIME: Joseph Smith is looking for something with his magic seeing stone. You decide by surrounding him with the treasures he found.

Ideas: Does he have the golden tablets? The angel Moroni might be looking over his shoulder. Is that a leprechaun behind a mushroom?

We have a knack for associating ideas and specific events with specific symbols. The cross represents Christians, the swastika represents Nazis, and the "swoosh" check-mark represents a shoe company. Regardless of whether or not the symbol was around a lot longer than the thing we associate with it, once we make the connection it's stuck. Don't be afraid of "sacred" symbols.

BONUS DOODLE TIME: Draw someone on the cross.

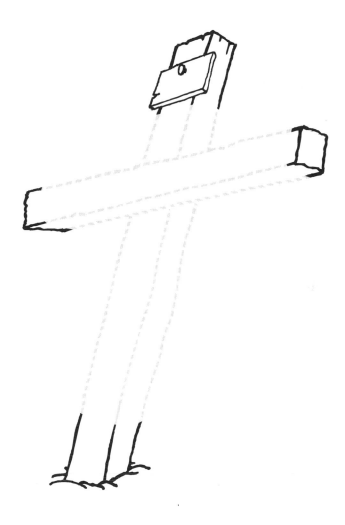

Tip: It could be a Jewish carpenter, a giant Easter bunny, Santa Claus, or a Cimmerian barbarian. Extra credit for adding other people on other crosses and coming up with a clever license plate at the top.

Spread the word
(or don't)

Chapter 5

When missionaries come calling, don't turn them away. Invite them in and be hospitable. (Be sure to have plenty of lemonade on hand because it's refreshing and caffeine free. They might be Mormons.[1]) Explain to them up front that you're an Atheist and there's no way they'll convince you to believe in their God, *but* that you're more than willing to talk about it with them. They will see this as a challenge of their faith-spreading abilities and you will become their Sunday project. They might even lose sleep over you.

This is an important part of being a good Atheist and serves several purposes. First, it shows the proselytistic[2] Christian that Atheists can be loving, caring people who are fun to talk to about religion. Second, you might gain new friends. And third, every minute they spend failing to convert you to their religion is a minute they aren't successfully converting someone else. After all, there are only so many minutes in a day.

---

1   Some Orthodox Mormons don't drink caffeine, while for others the rule prohibits hot drinks. Just to be safe, have a wide variety of drinks at the ready.

2   \pros'e li tis'tik\, adj.; Having the need or compulsion to convert another to one's religion. Of or having the need to recruit.

Who's that knocking on my door?

One time I was working in my garage and two men, an older one and a younger one, walked up and started talking to me in my driveway. They were wearing suits and casually held Bibles at their sides. The older man, Jim, spoke most while the younger man, whose name I forget, stood in the background and listened. At first it was friendly banter, then Jim started asking me my religious beliefs, if I had heard the good news, and if I would be interested in accepting Jesus Christ into my life. They said they would be happy to help me find salvation in my living room, with just a simple, life-affirming prayer session. I explained to them that I was an Atheist and wasn't interested in praying with them, but would gladly talk about religion with them.

They accepted my invitation and we began to discuss faith in the driveway. As I have experienced before, we quickly came to the impasse where they said they believed the Bible was divine truth and where I said I believed it was all made up and not divinely inspired, and the conversation couldn't go any further.

Jim asked if they could leave some literature (as they had more souls to save before the church van returned to the neighborhood to pick them up, I assumed), which I accepted. I told them that I was writing a book about being an Atheist and would share a copy with them when it was finished.

We agreed that the conversation had been lively and entertaining, and they said they would like to come back another time to talk some more and try to convince me to change my mind. I said they were always welcome and waved them farewell.

Later, when I examined their literature (a copy of *The Watch Tower* and a small book titled "THE BIBLE - God's Word or Man's?") I concluded that they were Jehovah's Witnesses. *The Watch Tower* is a Jehovah's Witness publication.

A few weeks later, they returned while I was out in the front yard and we talked again. Nothing really changed in the conversation and it ended quicker than the first time.

About a month after that the same two men came again. This time knocking on my front door. They brought me another book, titled, "You Can Live Forever in Paradise on Earth" and as we spoke through the screen door, they had a more urgent message, that my eternal soul was in danger, and more importantly, that my wife's eternal soul was in danger. They said this looking in the house, obviously looking *for* my wife to draw her into the conversation.

I stepped outside, shutting the door behind me and told them that their happy message from before was starting to sound like a threat. They didn't deny it, but said that they were worried for me. I told them that they were making me uncomfortable and frightening my wife, and that they should stop coming by to witness to me. They left, saying they would pray for me.

Ah, the joy of proselytizing. That's the warm gooey feeling you get when you tell someone that everything they've been taught about how the universe works is wrong and that they're going to be punished for all eternity if they don't accept what you say as the truth. It's fun (for you) and frightening (for them).

Spread the word, brothers and sisters, get out there and save some souls! If you don't, there's a good chance you might not get into heaven, either. Sounds like a threat to me, but some biblical literalists and old-fashioned evangelicals think that's what Christianity is all about. Spreading the word.

I don't mean to pick on the Christians, here. It's just that Christian missionaries are the ones I'm the most familiar with, and the only religious people who have ever actively tried to make me believe what they believe (back to the original reason I'm writing this book and the person for whom I'm writing it). Though I've known members of many faiths, I have never had one of my Jewish, Muslim,

Hindu, New Age, Pagan or Buddhist friends try to convince me to turn my back on what I believe and join his or her religion. The closest any of them have come to that is when a Buddhist friend of mine said I could be a member of any religion (even an Atheist) and still be a Buddhist, which was pretty appealing. But I have had plenty of Christians do it. They've come to my door, evangelicals, Jehovah's Witnesses, friends, family, Mormons, and more. Even teenagers have come knocking, asking me to give them money so they can go to Bible camp! I declined to make a donation.

The mission mentality makes perfect sense, whether it's religion or politics. If you can get everybody to believe the same thing you believe, you will have defeated your competition, they'll do whatever you want, you won't have anyone competing for your power base, and everyone will live in harmony. Plus, from a tribal perspective, if we have the same religion or the same politics, we'll all be a little closer to being in the same tribe and less likely to break off and start our own.

In the Village

The old man and his daughter squatted over the stew pot in the one room of their thatched-roof mud hut. They thanked their ancestors for the boiled carrots and cabbage and asked that the bland fare give them strength and nourishment. The daughter poured an ample portion for her father, handed him the bowl and asked, "How was your day, father?"

He sipped the broth and nodded his approval. "Fine," he said. "We drove away the yak without anyone getting hurt. It took all day, since we had to usher him far enough away to make sure he wouldn't come back. Good news, though, your uncle has asked me to go into the forest with him tomorrow to collect ginger root."

The old man was the best wild herb hunter in the village. The daughter smiled, "Uncle chose wisely to ask you."

The daughter sampled her own bowl of soup and wished she had some salt to add to it. She felt guilty then, knowing her father worked hard to afford the carrots and that he had salvaged the cabbage from the garden he kept behind the hut. It wasn't his fault the yak had strayed into their village and devoured every garden. He had even shared some of the vegetables he saved with neighbors who were less fortunate. She closed her eyes while she took another sip and silently thanked her ancestors for guarding some of the cabbage from the yak.

"Perhaps we will find enough ginger for me to buy you some salt and tarragon at the market," the old man said with a twinkle in his eye.

The daughter blushed. He knew her so well and took such good care of her. Ever since her mother and brother had died three years ago when the fever came to their village, he had made extra efforts to be kind and affectionate toward her. Before the fever, it had been her mother's job to cuddle and cajole the children. Now it was just the two of them and what was left of the village. He gladly took the added responsibility.

She didn't worry about her father. He was strong, worked hard to keep the thatched roof over their heads, and was well respected by the village as a good, moral man. Several neighbor widows would gladly share their huts with him after another year or so of mourning.

They sipped their dinner in relative silence. When they finished the pot, the daughter cleaned up while the old man added fuel to the fire.

"Have you seen the strange man?" the old man asked.

"Yes," the daughter answered, "he is pale and dresses oddly."

"Have you spoken with him?"

"No." She knew it would be imprudent to speak to a stranger without one of her parents present to protect her and her reputation.

The old man leaned toward her and gently touched her ankle. The gesture conveyed a simple message, these words are important. She sat up and gave her father her full attention.

"He has come here to change our lives."

She smiled, "In a good way?"

The old man shrugged. "He may bring us gifts, and he may bring us books and stories."

She smiled wider at the thought of gifts and stories. But her father didn't seem very excited about this prospect.

"He may also bring medicine," he said matter-of-factly.

The glow of her smile dimmed. She didn't like medicine, with its sharp needles and alkaline pills. When the fever had crept out of the forest and settled over the village, people wearing masks came with medicine. Everyone was given a painful inoculation that made their bellies ache and their arms sore for days. The medicine did not save her mother or her brother.

"More importantly," he said in his most sever tone, "he will bring us a message and a promise. Do you remember what your grandfather taught you about promises?"

She nodded. "If a man promises me a cow, don't believe him unless the cow is tied to a tree where I can see it."

"And if he promises you a chicken?"

She smiled, "Make sure it lays eggs."

"And if he promises you a bowl that is empty?"

"Then don't drink, because it won't serve me well to swallow emptiness."

The old man smiled with pride and winked at his sweet daughter. She was smart and self-directed, with a deep memory, and the wits to solve any problem. It wouldn't be long before she would be sharing a hut with a husband of her own.

"What will the man's message be?" the daughter asked, intrigued.

He thought about the answer, trying to craft his words in a way that wouldn't frighten her. Finally, he leaned back, relaxed, and posed a question.

"What do we have?"

"Each other," she said with a smile.

"And beyond that?" he asked, looking around the room.

"We have our home and our garden, the village and the forest, and the ancestors and the seasons."

"And what is beyond the forest?"

"Other villages and other forests."

"Do the people in the other villages have the same ancestors as we do?"

"Grandfather said that their ancestors' ancestors' ancestors come from the same village as our ancestors. Don't they?" The daughter was enjoying such a spirited conversation.

"Yes, but I mean our ancestors, here. The ones that watch us and laugh with us and show us where to find ginger root. Are they the same ancestors as the other village?"

"No. Our village was grandfather's village, and he and his uncles and aunts live here with us. And in the forest."

The old man scratched his chin. "Should we go to other villages and tell them they should thank our grandfather for the seasons instead of their own grandfather?"

The daughter thought before answering. Her grandfather had been a powerful man and as a spirit always guided them wisely. She knew that if he wanted to help somebody else, even somebody far away, he could do it effortlessly. But she didn't think it would be in his nature to leave their village to help another. Plus, it didn't feel right to her, the thought of telling another village which ancestors to call upon.

"No," she said finally, "that doesn't seem right."

The old man nodded.

"When I was a boy," he said, "much younger than you are now, a stranger came to our village. He brought us gifts and stories."

"And a promise?"

"Yes, a promise. He held out a bowl of promise to us that was wonderful and happy. He told us that the whole world would be ours if we drank from his bowl, and all we needed to give in return was our ancestors and our way of life."

"Give?" She leaned forward with concern.

"He wanted us to turn our backs on the ancestors and ignore them. Neither talk to them nor listen to them, ever again."

"How lonely that would make them!" she cried out, "and how

sad! Was the bowl empty?"

"Yes. But luckily," he said with a smile, "we didn't drink from his bowl, so we didn't fill ourselves with the emptiness. And we kept grandfather and his uncles with us."

The daughter heaved a sigh of relief and rocked back on her heels. Then she furrowed her brow and crossed her arms with a pout. "I don't want this man's gifts or his stories, if they come at such a price."

"There's more," the old man ventured, testing the waters of her emotional endurance. "Would you like to hear it?" She nodded.

"With his promise came a threat."

Her eyes grew wide. "A threat?"

"The man said that if we turned down the bowl he offered, we would be punished."

"Punished? Would he beat you?"

"No. He said that when we died we wouldn't get to stay here in the village or walk in the forest. He said we would live in a lake of fire and forever boil there like carrots and cabbage in a stew!"

Still wide-eyed, the daughter pressed the old man, "Boil in a lake of fire?"

He nodded solemnly. "Forever."

She thought about it for a while, frowning, mulling the images over in her mind's eye. Finally, she looked at her father.

"Well, that's just silly," she said emphatically.

The old man laughed heartily. "It is," he said.

She slapped her thigh, "I bet grandfather thought it was silly, too."

"He did."

The old man hugged his daughter to his chest with more pride that night than he had ever felt for her and rocked back and forth. For a while they basked in the fading glow of the fire, until there was a knock at the entrance to their hut. The old man stepped outside.

The daughter heard words of greeting. The tone was respectful and calm, so she hurried to put another pot of water on the fire. There were some herb leaves and flower petals in the tea gourd, which she dropped into the pot. Then she found several cups that her father had carved from the knots of trees. She lined them up, dusted them off, and picked the most impressive four. She was uncertain how many visitors were outside, or how many guests might be invited in, but she couldn't imagine more than four adults being able to sit comfortably around the fire. Just as she was setting cups to one side of the pot, her father re-entered.

"How do we treat guests?" he whispered.

"With the respect we show our ancestors," she replied. "I've made tea."

The old man patted her cheek and looked sorrowfully at the empty tea gourd. When I am hunting for ginger root, I will have to remember to pick some fresh herbs tomorrow, he thought to himself.

"Please come in," he called to the door.

A city elder stepped through the entrance and smiled.

"Hello, daughter," he said.

"Hello, uncle," she responded politely.

Following closely behind the elder was the stranger. He was so tall he had to crouch to keep from bumping his head on the thatch. He looked around the room with unveiled surprise. Probably, she thought, because he has never seen so many beautifully carved cups as father's cups.

"I am pleased to meet you," the stranger said very formally, as if she were a married woman.

"Hello," she responded, not looking him directly in the eyes and keeping out of his reach.

The old man invited his guests to sit with him beside the fire. His daughter offered the stranger a cup.

"Please have some tea."

The stranger glanced at the elder, who nodded. He took the cup and sipped it. He was surprised by the rich flavor, smacked his lips and coughed.

The old man winked at her. She handed the village elder a cup and hurried out of his line of sight.

"Tea, uncle?"

"Thank you, daughter," he said. He sipped it and also smacked his lips. "Very fresh," he said hoarsely.

The old man took his cup and sat the polite way so that his daughter was slightly behind him.

"Welcome to our home," he said lifting his cup in toast. They all sipped then smacked their lips, relishing the sharp aftertaste.

The stranger produced from a fold in his clothing a small bundle of dry cloth wrapped with string.

"I present this gift to you, in friendship," he said, handing the packet to the old man.

The three villagers collectively oohed and aahed at such a grand gesture.

The old man turned the packet over in his hands, examining it closely as his daughter stared over his shoulder. He pinched a loose end of string and pulled the knot free. Then, savoring the anticipation, he slowly peeled back the folds until the contents lay in the palm of his hand.

"Father..." the daughter whispered in astonishment.

"Amazing," the old man said, looking at the sand-colored lump of salt in his palm. It was a treasure; as much as he would buy in an entire year.

"My thanks, friend," he said to the stranger, a little nervous to have such a commodity. "I should break this into smaller pieces to share it with all of my neighbors!" He reached for a shaving stone but the village elder stopped him.

"No need," the elder said. "Our new friend will give each house in the village a similar gift."

"Such riches!" the old man said. He could hardly imagine the wealth one must have to be so generous. He bowed to the stranger, "thank you for this most generous gift."

Compliments were exchanged, followed by polite conversation. The old man and the daughter learned that the village elders agreed to let the stranger live in their village for some time, maybe several years. He was looking for volunteers to help him build a school for the children, despite the fact that the forest was a reputable school already. He was also planning to build an expansive hut so large that the entire village could gather there for meetings.

The daughter exclaimed that such a building would surely be a feat of architectural wonder.

The stranger told them that in the gathering hut and school they would learn new ways to grow their gardens, sing songs, and meet other strangers like him who would teach them many things to make their lives better and help them live longer. They would teach the villagers how to survive without hunting and gathering in the forest.

The elder explained that the stranger was going to live in their village and travel out from there to visit other neighboring villages, taking salt with him and building huts for gathering. He said the stranger chose their village because of its special status, the wisdom of its elders and its location. The stranger had even given it a name: The Heart of the Enemy.

The old man and his daughter smiled proudly that their village earned such a distinction.

When their cups were empty and the fire began to sputter, the elder signaled that it soon would be time to go. The stranger thanked the old man for his hospitality and thanked the daughter for the tea.

"Before I depart this evening," the stranger said, "may I ask you a question?"

Here comes the bowl, the old man thought. He raised an eyebrow to his daughter over his shoulder and politely responded, "Of course. Please do."

The stranger's countenance became grave. He hesitated as if the question was of utmost importance, his pale blue eyes searching the depths of the old man's charcoal black eyes. He took a deep breath and offered a generous, giving smile as he let it out.

"Have you heard the good news?"

Why should you spread the word?

I can think of two answers.

1. Because I love of my fellow man and have a sincere desire to save him.

2. Because I want to eliminate the enemies of my religion (other religions).

This goes back to where I said that the idea of religion is wonderful until you add the human element. I'm sure most missions start out with number 1, a love of their fellow man and the sincere desire to save him. But as soon as you add the politics of "our religion against their religion" you slide into Number 2 and find yourself in a struggle to eliminate the enemy.

Caca. I know of an American couple that became missionaries and moved to Cambodia as part of a long-term goal to spread Christianity throughout the country. Their outward motivation was simple and pure: educate, glorify God and save people who were ignorant of His grace. But there was an underlying plot to their mission. Just beneath the surface was the desire to eliminate a culture and a religion. Or, to incorporate evangelical Christian beliefs into the culture while replacing the existing religion. Their rationale was to take a people wallowing in the stagnant waters of moral poverty and raise them up with education, fellowship, and happy songs they could play on the guitar.

So if you have an urge to share your faith, ask yourself what it is you're actually feeling. Is it really an act of generosity? Or is it because you think that your faith is the only true faith? If your faith is the only true faith, you probably believe that other religions are either innocent, ignorant mistakes or they are the work of the Devil, designed to trick and trap people into damnation. Think about it from someone else's point of view. If you believe that any religion other than your own is Satanism, couldn't the same be said for your religion? If a Baptist thinks Roman Catholics are idol worshipers, and Catholics think Baptists are apostates[3], which one is right? If a Christian thinks a Muslim is a Satan worshiper, and a Muslim thinks a Christian is an infidel, how can they reach a compromise without destroying each other or destroying each other's religion?

My writing partner and I once came up with a stage play wherein the Devil, disguised as the most popular kid in college, explained to his Jewish freshman roommate that he had invented Christianity to lure the chosen people (Jews) away from God.

Within Christianity alone, think of all the different denominations. Some thinking the others are false, idolaters, Satanists, heretics, or just plain wrong. Sometimes a denomination will split over the smallest disagreement, like which direction to dip someone during baptism, or how many times they have to be submerged in order to fully maximize their Holy Spirit saturation.

I was curious how many different denominations there are, so I performed a simple Yahoo!© search on the Internet for "christian denominations" and this was the first list that was returned:

African Methodist Episcopal
African Methodist Episcopal Zion
African Orthodox Church
American Baptist Churches USA
Amish
Anabaptist
Anglican Catholic Church
Antiochian Orthodox
Armenian Evangelical Church
Armenian Orthodox
Assemblies of God
Associated Gospel Churches of Canada
Association of Vineyard Churches
Baptist
Baptist Bible Fellowship
Branch Davidian

---

3   \apostate\, n.; One who has relinquished one's religious faith, one's principles, or has given up a cause.

Brethren in Christ
Bruderhof Communities
Byzantine Catholic Church
Calvary Chapel
Calvinist
Catholic
Cell Church
Celtic Orthodox
Charismatic Episcopal Church
Children of God (COG)
Christadelphian
Christian and Missionary Alliance
Christian Churches of God
Christian Identity
Christian Reformed Church
Christian Science
Church of God (Anderson)
Church of God (Cleveland)
Church of God (Seventh Day)
Church of God in Christ
Church of God of Prophecy
Church of Jesus Christ of Latter-day Saints
Church of Scotland
Church of South India
Church of the Brethren
Church of the Lutheran Brethren of America
Church of the Nazarene
Church of the New Jerusalem
Church of the United Brethren in Christ
Church Universal and Triumphant
Churches of Christ
Churches of God General Conference
Congregational Christian Churches
Coptic Orthodox
Cumberland Presbyterian Church
Disciples of Christ
Episcopal
Ethiopian Orthodox Tewahedo Church
Evangelical Congregational Church
Evangelical Covenant Church
Evangelical Formosan Church
Evangelical Free Church

Evangelical Lutheran Church
Evangelical Methodist Church
Evangelical Presbyterian
Fellowship of Christian Assemblies
Fellowship of Grace Brethren
Fellowship of Independent Evangelical Churches
Free Church of Scotland
Free Methodist
Free Presbyterian
Free Will Baptist
Gnostic
Great Commission Association of Churches
Greek Orthodox Hutterian Brethren
Independent Fundamental Churches of America
Indian Orthodox
International Church of the Foursquare Gospel
International Churches of Christ
Jehovah's Witnesses
Living Church of God
Local Church
Lutheran
Lutheran Church - Missouri Synod
Mar Thoma Syrian Church
Mennonite
Messianic Judaism
Methodist
Moravian Church
Nation of Yahweh
New Frontiers International
Old Catholic Church
Orthodox
Orthodox Church in America
Orthodox Presbyterian
Pentecostal
Plymouth Brethren
Presbyterian
Presbyterian Church (USA)
Presbyterian Church in America
Primitive Baptist
Protestant Reformed Church
Reformed
Reformed Baptist

Reformed Church in America
Reformed Church in the United States
Reformed Churches of Australia
Reformed Episcopal
Reformed Presbyterian Church
Reorganized Church of Jesus Christ of Latter Day Saints
Revival Centres International
Romanian Orthodox
Rosicrucian
Russian Orthodox
Serbian Orthodox
Seventh Day Baptist
Seventh-Day Adventist
Shaker
Society of Friends
Southern Baptist Convention
Spiritist
Syrian Orthodox
True and Living Church of Jesus Christ of Saints of the Last Days
Two-by-Twos
Unification Church
Unitarian-Universalism
United Church of Canada
United Church of Christ
United Church of God
United Free Church of Scotland
United Methodist Church
United Reformed Church
Uniting Church in Australia
Unity Church
Unity Fellowship Church
Universal Fellowship of Metropolitan Community Churches
Virtual Churches
Waldensian Church
Wesleyan
Wesleyan Methodist
Worldwide Church of God

Are all 137 of these right and true because they call themselves
Christians? I'm sure some denominations think the others are on the
wrong track and probably can't get into heaven with their beliefs.

The "Primitive Baptist" name intrigues me. I can't help but imagine people swathed in deerskin, dunking each other in the hot springs near the tar pits.

OK, let's say you're a Christian. What's the definition of a Christian? Who is Christ? If you believe in the Catholic Christ, but don't believe he did the things that the Latter Day Saints attribute to him, does that mean you're worshipping different Christs? If you can each worship different Christs and yet both still be Christians, does that mean that Hindus who believe that Christ was an incarnation of Krishna are also Christians?

My mother believes that every religion was put on Earth by God to meet the needs of the people, based on their geography and culture. She says that since the Jewish religion wouldn't work for the eskimos, He gave the eskimos a different way to worship Him. No better, no worse, and just as valid as the other faiths. There are a lot of people in the world that believe in that Pluralist outlook. The fundamentalists I'm talking about, though, think that's a bunch of heathen bunk.

My missionary position

If your goal as a missionary is to teach people how to grow food, to bring them medicine and proper hygiene, to teach them how to use computers, and to teach them how to take care of themselves, why do you need to insert your religion into the mix? That couple in Cambodia raised money on the pretext that they would be helping people, making their lives better. In one of their first messages back to America, they mentioned that they were going to Siem Reap (or maybe Battambang), a city that had so many Buddhist temples that it "was surely Satan's stronghold in Cambodia." This revealed their intentions to me. They weren't going to Cambodia to help the poor. Their goal was to destroy Buddhism there by planting the seed of dissillusionment. Or that was at least part of their mission, along with helping the poor.

Someone else's culture may not be the healthiest lifestyle, or offer them the greatest opportunities for scientific advancement, but it is still their culture. I think you can do plenty of good in this world, in your own neighborhood as well as on another continent, without injecting your religion into someone else's culture.

A Christian friend of mine told me that the general belief in his church is that if someone has never heard the "Good News" that Christ died for their sins, then God won't punish them when they die, regardless of the pagan or heathen lifestyle they live. If they haven't heard The Word, they don't go to hell.

Then why would they ever want to hear The Word?

Someone asked a preacher that if God is a merciful and loving god, then what happens in the afterlife to all the "natives," that lived and died all over the world, before the missions came to town. Did he punish them for never having heard the story of Jesus Christ? Doesn't seem fair. So that preacher gave the heathens a Get Out of Hell Free card and said that God wouldn't punish people who had never heard The Word. And it stuck.

Of course, evangelicals just can't keep their mouths shut about it (because they won't go to heaven if they do), so they go all over the globe, spreading The Word like a virus, and guaranteeing the damnation of all those who hear the story, but choose not to accept Jesus Christ as their personal savior. They can't just leave them in ignorance and let them into heaven through God's back door.

When missionaries first arrived in the New World, they had to devise ways to communicate without words while they learned the native tongue. Some preferred pantomime while others delivered their message with art. Still, others used **biological warfare** to spread their message of a wrathful God.

DOODLE TIME: Tell a biblical story with art. Complete the tale of David and Goliath by adding the details.

Tips: show the hordes of troops on either side, use a red pen to surround Goliath's body in a pool of his blood, and give David a thick, curly head of hair (and maybe some pants).

Know thine enemy

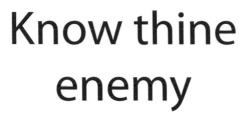

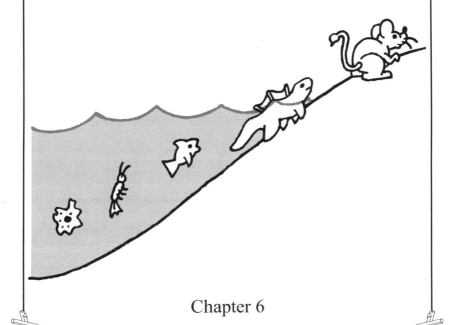

Chapter 6

To be the best Atheist you can be, you need to know your enemy, the people that want to convince you that you're wrong. Learn their methods for explaining away your concerns. Also, be aware of their fear and intimidation tactics.

There's always the threat of hell. It's scary and a powerful enough image to convince anyone to drop to their knees and beg for God's grace. If you argue that it's an illogical threat, they'll remind you that God's ways are not our ways and that God doesn't reason the way we reason. Don't even try to argue the point. It's not worth your time or consternation.

They'll use the twisted logic that "if you're not with us, you're against us," that only thoughts and deeds inspired by [whoever they worship] can be good. All the rest comes from the devil. And that you can't know peace unless you know [whoever they worship]. They'll say that all the happy, peaceful Atheists out there are just fooling themselves and can't really be happy.

Hate the sin, but love the sinner

If you haven't heard it before, you're bound to eventually. Unfortunately, there are a lot of evangelicals out there who prefer to live by a different mantra: "hate the sin, hate the sinner, love the sin they don't catch you doing yourself." Hypocrisy runs rampant in the fundamentalist Christian world. Keep that in mind and never assume that someone who calls himself or herself a Christian isn't going to screw you royally. They're just people, and they're as full of greed, pride and hate as everyone else. They have egos, tempers, and are motivated by physical need.

Also, never fall into the trap of thinking that kind, loving or highly educated people aren't extremely close-minded and intolerant. There are forces beyond your control making them think the way they think. And sometimes, if they need to hurt you financially, emotionally, or even physically to get you to believe the way they believe, don't think it's beyond them to do it.

Trust your gut. Most people are good, but stay cautious, especially once they know you're an Atheist.

Since a literalist thinks everything in the Bible is true (even things that contradict each other) they can pull any quote and say it's true. God is jealous. The walls of Jericho were blown down by priests blowing their horns and Israelites shouting at the city. Jesus walked on water. Noah lived to be over 700 years old.

I wonder how many of the world's ills today would be solved if people stopped thinking the Bible, Torah, and Koran are (separately) literal truth. If everyone saw them for what they are, figurative stories and guides for living peacefully in a man-made society, there would be a lot less for people of different faiths and cultures to argue about, or kill each other over.

GE 1:27 So God created man in his own image, in the image of God he created him; male and female he created them.

GE 2:7 the LORD God formed the man from the dust of the ground and breathed into his nostrils the breath of life, and the man became a living being.

Lots of people believe the story that a lump of clay, a keen eye for sculpting, and some magic breath was the recipe for the grandparents of all humanity. In fact, there are more people who believe in the story of creation than people who don't. That doesn't mean it's true, only that more people have been scammed by superstition and the churches than those who haven't.

Some people claim that Genesis 2:7 is a metaphor for all life coming from the basic elements. But this isn't about metaphor; it's about the literalists who believe that we are all descended from two people who were handcrafted by God out of Play-doh.

When someone tells me that Genesis 2:7 is the literal truth, I ask them that if God made Adam and Eve from scratch, why did he give Adam nipples? Does the first man need a vestigial[1] organ? And if Adam didn't have nipples, how did the rest of the men in the world develop them? I think it boils down to this: men have nipples because we evolved from an animal that either was strictly a single-gendered mammal (female only) or both genders breastfed the offspring. I think it might be the former.

I've heard it expressed that there is a stage in prenatal development where all fetuses are female. It's probably one of those urban myths, like the toddler who picked up the car his mother was trapped beneath, or the guy in turn-of-the-millennium Rome who fed five thousand men a hearty meal with only two fish and five loaves of bread. Of course, if you look at our chromosomes, it makes more sense to believe that we came from a creature that didn't have separate genders. Everything you need to make a human is in the X chromosome (notice that women only have X chromosomes). All the Y chromosome does is **change the genitals, make men grow body hair,** grunt, scratch, and inspire them to buy tickets to monster truck rallies.

Why do we grow wisdom teeth? What's the purpose of our appendix? Why did God give men foreskin if He just wanted them to chop it off? The evidence against the literal acceptance of the Bible is all

---

1   Vestigial is when a body part becomes useless because of evolutionary change. It means rudimentary, or small due to lack of use. Whales have vestigial hip bones and feet, which imply they once had legs.

around us, all over us, and inside us. I even wrote a poem about it. My ode to the appendix. Please don't mail me one.

VESTIGIAL PARTS

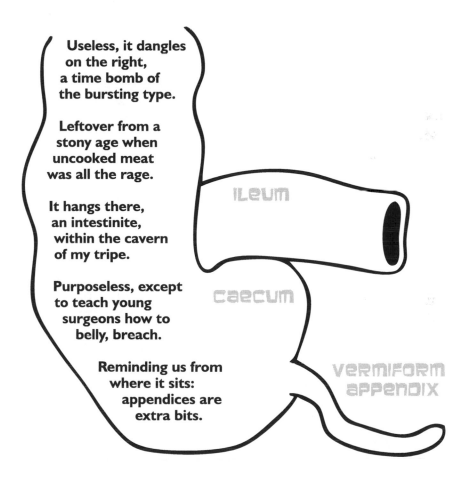

Useless, it dangles
on the right,
a time bomb of
the bursting type.

Leftover from a
stony age when
uncooked meat
was all the rage.

It hangs there,
an intestinite,
within the cavern
of my tripe.

Purposeless, except
to teach young
surgeons how to
belly, breach.

Reminding us from
where it sits:
appendices are
extra bits.

ILeum

caecum

Vermiform
appendix

I'd like someone to make it into a song with a thumping, digestive beat. I can picture the music video being animated with a chorus line of happy, dancing organs. Everything is fine until the appendix slows down, turns red, and starts to swell. It stumbles through the chorus line, getting in the way of the other organs and being chased around by white blood cells, getting bigger and redder until it eventually explodes, spewing septic bile all over the other body parts. And then the whole production comes to a crashing, heart-stopping end. Maybe just the whine of the EKG's flatline trailing off as it fades to black.

Then Why Do I Have Toenails?

The congregation finishes the hymn and takes their seats. It's 8:35 a.m., the first scheduled sermon of the Sabbath. A few stragglers shuffle in and find places in the rear. A nervous silence falls over them as they wait for Pastor Jay Johnson, who is curiously absent. He had not led them in the first song of praise.

The marquee in front of the church is clearly visible from the street for all to see. It is ideal for clever, thought-provoking messages about the wages of sin and how rush hour drivers can only know peace if they know Jesus. Also, its proximity to the sidewalk and low profile meant that Pastor Jay could easily change the message without climbing on a ladder and testing his conviction about what the afterlife has in store for him.

Members of the congregation fidget slightly, clear their throats, and otherwise make an effort to avoid eye contact with each other, lest they strike up a conversation about the subject of their worry. Friday afternoon the letters on the marquee had changed abruptly from a message of inspiration to one of an ominous nature. Some of them stared at the Burning Bush to one side of the altar.

Aptly named, the Burning Bush is a wrought iron piece of art shaped like a perfectly symmetrical tumbleweed just before a strong wind sends it rolling across the plains. Set atop a large iron bowl, the Burning Bush was a fanciful bar-b-que grill in a past life that some parishioner donated to the church. Pastor Jay, eager to put all donations to good use, had removed the wheels, scraped off the "I like pork" bumper sticker, and christened the contraption with a fresh coat of outdoor, fire-resistant paint. Typically reserved for church picnics by the volleyball sand pit, today it stands opposite the pulpit, glowing brightly with blue propane-fueled fire.

Jay Johnson peers out from the wings at the congregation: a full house. He smiles at his cleverness. There had been anxious discussions at recent adult Bible study classes about the book. "What will it do to the fragile minds of the children who might read it?" One parent proudly announced that she had forbidden her child's social studies teacher from using the abominable work in her course study. Another parishioner claimed that the devil had crawled out of the book, into her husband and made him question his faith. She assured the group, though, that some extra prayer just before bed and a calculated degree of abstinence on her part had successfully driven the devil out of him.

These concerns were worrisome enough for Pastor Jay to address the congregation about the book. It was always a touchy subject, condemning a book, what with free speech and all. It had been easy for that children's book about witchcraft and wizardry, sure, but this book? He had to quell the fears of the more sensitive parishioners without driving away the literate members. At all costs, the sermon would have to keep members, and more importantly keep their tithes and other donations flowing into the coffers.

He decided to address the subject of creation versus evolution. It was an old argument without a clear winner. As he liked to put it, it was a debate between the theory of evolution and the truth of creation. He had a metal decal on the hatchback of his Ford Escort that clearly stated the same by showing a small Darwin fish (an outline of a fish, with feet, surrounding the name DARWIN) being devoured by a larger, footless fish outline, filled with the word, TRUTH. To bring in the congregation this week, he had changed the marquee from, "Love thy neighbor, but don't be IN love with thy neighbor" to

"Why I am an Atheist. Thoughts about faith."

A sermon by Pastor Jay Johnson, ThD.

Pastor Jay takes a breath, makes sure the lavaliere microphone attached below the second button of his shirt is switched "on," and strides out of the wings to face the congregation. In his hand he holds a copy of the offending subject matter. A narrow paperback book with a bright blue cover.

All eyes are on Pastor Jay and what he holds as he walks past the pulpit to face the congregation. One of the older female members actually gasps. In a deft act of intimacy he casually sits on the top step of the dais and rests the book on his knee. He turns to a dog-eared page of the book and reads, "If God created me in his image, then why do I have toenails?" paraphrasing the word "nipples" to "toenails," to protect the more delicate members.

Pastor Jay hangs his head, shaking it slightly, and stands. He turns to the colorful tapestry of a cup and dove hanging above the altar, where in another time a carving of a sorrowful, bloody Jesus would be nailed to a cross and staring up at the ceiling imploring the heavens to end His misery. Jay shrugs as he lifts the book, and addresses the tapestry, "Why do I have toenails?"

He slowly turns to the congregation as he continues, "could it have been in God's plan to give me toenails just so I could scratch the back of my calf? Or are toenails a sign, no, proof that we are descended from some other animal? A creature that used its feet to climb trees, dig in the dirt, and defend itself? The Bible tells us that God created us in his image and that he crafted Adam from the dust and the clay, then made Eve from one of Adam's ribs. If that didn't happen, then is the rest of the Bible also false?"

The congregation stares wide-eyed at him. He slowly drops his arms to his sides and hangs his head again, like a man who has given up, to let his words sink in to the hundreds perched on the edges of their pews. "Could toenails mean that God didn't do what the Bible says?"

Seemingly without thinking about it, clever Pastor Jay lifts a foot and scratches the calf of his other leg with the toe of his loafer. A sigh of relief and a chorus of laughter rains from the congregation. He raises his head, smiling, and tosses the book on the Burning Bush. It curls and blackens over the fire as smoke from its pages is carried into the vaulted rafters by the church's air-conditioning.

The band leader cues a lively beat and the choir joins in with "Old Time Religion." Back to business, Pastor Jay says to himself as he walks to the pulpit.

Despite all the evidence before us that evolution occurs in the world, there are still people who want to hide from it or ignore the facts.

DOODLE TIME: Have fun with the idea of us crawling out of
the muck to become a vicar. Add your own
evolutionary milestones.

Consider protozoa, invertebrates, fish, a creepy crawly thing that hauls
itself out of the water, and maybe a cute, rascally marsupial.

The sun revolves around the Earth

Chapter 7

People want to ignore that they're going to die. They'll do almost anything to avoid the thought, from having plastic surgery to believing in the afterlife. They'd go so far as to tell you that the world is flat, dinosaurs never roamed the planet, and that the universe is powered by love and a nurturing omniscience.

But if you're like me, you know better.

If the wages of sin and not accepting Jesus Christ as my personal savior leads to eternal damnation, then why aren't I afraid of going to Hell?

Here's the answer to the question about the existence of intelligent Atheists. First, assuming that I'm an intelligent Atheist is probably pushing it. I don't necessarily think I could prove that I'm intelligent. I'm just an Atheist. But I have faith in my intelligence. I can't prove it exists, but I'm certain it's there.

Earlier I wrote: I often find people asking me, "How can someone as smart as you not believe in God?"

Sometimes I play dumb and furrow my brow at them as I respond with a hillbilly drawl. But more often, my typical response is, "How can someone as smart as you believe in God?" Sometimes they respond to my question with, "Aren't you afraid of going to hell?" To which I say, "**If God is a loving, forgiving god, why would He punish me with eternal pain and suffering?**"

With a DUH expression on their faces, they answer, "Because the Bible says so." To which, I say, "But the Bible was written by men and isn't necessarily the truth."

That's when they kick me in the groin and the yelling begins.

When I tell my Christian friends that the Bible is a good book when it's used as a guideline for living, but that it's not the actual word of God, they typically respond that they believe the Bible was divinely inspired and that the men who wrote it were guided by God, which makes the book infallible. Then they tell me I'm going to hell.

I must not be an intelligent Atheist because the smart ones just keep their mouths shut and don't get kicked in the groin very often. The intelligent ones nod and smile and understand that to argue with the irrational is like arguing with a mad bull that wants to trample you. You can plead, "mister bull, I just want to cross this field instead of walking around it, I promise I won't eat your hay," all you want, but it isn't going to stop him from dancing on your ribcage. Better to avoid than to risk the confrontation.

How can someone as smart as you believe in God?

Earlier I described what I consider the evolution of the concept of an afterlife. It boils down to people believing that good people go to heaven and bad people go to hell. Since most of us consider ourselves "good" we need the promise that there's a place we get to go after we die where we don't suffer. It makes us happy and free of regret for not achieving as much as possible in this lifetime. It also helps us face our own mortality with less anxiety. Likewise, the thought of an afterlife where we are judged keeps most of us from breaking the really big laws during our lifetimes, and assures us that the really bad people will be punished for their crimes.

A few years ago, I went to visit an uncle who was dying of cancer. We knew it would be the last time we saw each other. He was tired of the pain and suffering he had endured for the past decade as the cancer slowly devoured him. I sat next to him in his home-hospice room for a little while, talking with him. When I got up to leave, I couldn't help but tell him we would see each other again. I really didn't believe it, but it was the kind of comfort I thought he needed just days before he died.

My true Christian friends believe that it takes more than "being good" to get into heaven. Different Christian groups have different litmus tests, but they effectively boil down to giving your life to Jesus, believing that He was the only begotten son of God, and that he died for our sins and was resurrected.

Where do we go?

So, people I know who believe in an afterlife or in some cases multiple afterlives, wonder what I believe happens to us when the Grim Reaper comes a-calling. I tell them, "nothing."

Have you ever awoken from a dreamless sleep? From the moment you fell asleep to the instant you woke up, you can't remember anything. There were no dreams, no self-awareness, and no gray area between sleep and wakefulness. Now imagine if there was no waking from that condition. It wouldn't matter because you're not aware that you're lying there having dreamless sleep.

That's what I believe death is like. I expect to just stop. The lights will go out and it will be over.

It's a little frightening at first to consider it, because we have a difficult time accepting an end to our own consciousness. But all through life we get little tastes of it every time we wake up in the morning and can't remember anything after falling asleep the night before.

Full of soul

We have a certain amount of energy in us. Electro-chemical impulses leap across our synapses, sending signals to and from our brains. My father told me once that he wonders where this energy goes when we die. He wonders if it just dissipates into the atmosphere and joins the rest of the ambient energy floating around. Is that energy our soul? Is it the spark of life in our eyes that fades when we die? There's no way to know until it happens, so I don't worry about it. Everybody dies. Everybody who has ever lived has died. And everybody who will ever live, will one day die, so I'm not scared of what's to come for me, since more people than I can imagine have experienced the exact same thing.

If I'm going to spend eternity in a hell with my peers, I'm prepared to do that. If you consider that many Christians believe that Catholics (including Mother Theresa), Mormons, Ghandi, and Buddhists are going to Hell, I'll be in good company. Of course, there won't be a whole lot of time for conversation, what with the pitchforks, wailing, brimstone, and unmentionable sexual torture we'll be afflicted with, 24/7. Maybe we'll get an occasional break from the torture, during which I'll ask Mother Theresa if this is what she expected.

If the universe is a nurturing place, then why don't I feel nurtured?

A good friend of mine believes the universe is a nurturing place full of love, kindness, and guidance. He asks me, "How can we feel love without there being a loving God?" He doesn't accept existence without some type of design or purpose driving it, and he doesn't accept a design or purpose that isn't built on the foundation of love. In his opinion, the universe is full of love; a great big nanny who tucks us in at night and tells us tomorrow is going to be a better day. It's like a giant, invisible, all-knowing Mrs. Garrett from *The Facts of Life.*

I don't blame him. It's a frightening thought to be all alone without purpose and without the safety net of an infinitely merciful guardian watching over us.

I have to disagree with him, though. I believe the universe is a cold, heartless wasteland devoid of life, intelligence and design. There's nothing nurturing about it. And the only things in abundance in the universe are space, magnificent cataclysm, and an infinitely large sense of ironic humor.

What else could be the explanation for sentient life popping up on a tiny planet in an unremarkable solar system at the very edge of a nondescript galaxy floating around with a bunch of other nondescript galaxies like pre-pubescent skateboarders loitering outside of a 7-Eleven, smoking cigarettes and talking about how they're going to "make it" one day after they escape from the oppression of their parents' house and get their yet-to-be-drawn underground comic book published?

The big bad universe is going to get me

Beyond a narrow, two-mile deep blanket of air, tucked between two relatively close latitudes on the surface of our planet, the universe holds nothing for us except discomfort and death. It's an impossibly narrow envelope of comfort that lets us live, breathe, reproduce, and evolve into our full potential. If we ascend above the safety zone for an extended amount of time, we freeze in the Arctic, we die for lack of oxygen above a certain altitude, or we explosively decompress in the vacuum of space. If we descend below the safety zone, we freeze in the Antarctic, we die for lack of oxygen under water, or the vast weight of the ocean crushes us.

Have you ever feared for your life

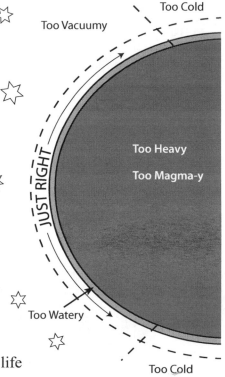

Too Cold

Too Vacuumy

Too Heavy

Too Magma-y

JUST RIGHT

Too Watery

Too Cold

doing nothing, like swimming in the ocean, walking around during a thunderstorm, climbing too high up a tree, or staring into the eyes of a rottweiler that has ignored its shock collar and volunteered to broaden the boundaries of its "Beware of Dog" sign onto the deserted country road in which you find yourself standing? That feeling you experience swimming at the beach when you can no longer see the shore is the universe trespassing into your safety zone. Every sunburn, winter sniffle, growling dog and roll of thunder is the universe reminding you that you're a temporary resident in an FBI safe house, and it is the unquenchable thirst of mafia vengeance one week before the trial where you intend to testify against The Boss. You're a goner.

Maybe that analogy is too harsh. Here's how I like to describe the universe and our place in it. The universe is a raging, class five whitewater river. It rushes downstream, crashing over the tops of slick, jagged rocks, hurtling into bends, and cascading over precipitous waterfalls. And yet despite the river's destructive nature, you find a calm spot in the river behind a rock, where plants and fish are safe from the maelstrom. That's Earth at this point in time in the mighty Rio Universo. We're the fish.

We swim around in the calm while the river rushes past us, mere inches away. Some rocks have calm pools behind them while others have nothing but frothy death. Does the fish think the existence of its pool is the product of some benevolent design, or just dumb luck? Probably neither, since it's a fish and doesn't ponder such things. I believe the fact that there's a calm spot in the raging river where fish and plants can exist in relative peacefulness is nothing more than coincidence.

So the universe is an awful place filled with freezing cold emptiness, space dust stretched out between bursts of stars colliding, and resonating with the high-pitched squeal of matter being crushed into the nothingness of black holes. That's not to say it's not a fun place to live, though. Who cares if it's dangerous and destructive? As long as we have some plants to nibble on and nothing disturbs the tranquility of our calm spot in the river, we should keep swimming around in circles with smiles on our fishy faces.

I don't think it's a bad thing that the universe is so dangerous. It's just reality; incomprehensibly beautiful, magnificently scary reality. The best way to endure it is to push the magnificently scary side of the universe away and relish the incomprehensibly beautiful side. Stop and watch a pretty sunset, even if its rich colors are the byproduct of pollution or a warning sign that a hurricane is coming.

If God put it all together for us, why not make more of the planet habitable? Is it to teach us to work with what we have? Knowing our potential for exploration and ingenuity, why is Earth the only habitable planet in our solar system? Why not make ten Earths for us to spread out to, and worship Him from? Or is that our job? You could counter that we have the brains to make Mars habitable, so the lesson is, "if it's worth having, it's worth working hard for." Well, I'll give you that, it makes a little sense. But I still think it's a stretch.

Islands and continents surrounded by oceans might seem as much a challenge to Stone Age people as space travel seems to us, but at least once they crossed the gulf they could breathe on the other side. Putting even potentially habitable planets light-years away from each other smacks of coincidence, not some greater plan for building our collective character.

I dream of black widow spiders

She's beautiful isn't she? Sleek, shiny, symmetrical, and the deepest black you can imagine. That perfect bright red hourglass on the underside of her belly tells you that if you get too close, your time may run out. There she is, hunkered down in a dark, safe place, ready to pounce, spinning her maze-like web to catch dinner or a husband, or both. She is as much proof that the universe is a dangerous destructive place as anything. Please don't mail me one.

There is beauty in the most frightening aspects of our existence. Think about an active lava flow, a lightning storm, or a pride of lions on the savannah. All of them are frightening and wondrous. Just keep your distance.

Our demise, individually and universally, is unavoidable. Why spend the precious time we have here on Earth fretting over how or when it's going to end and worrying about what, if anything, follows? The fact that we feel something like love is the great unanswerable question. We should take advantage of having it; we can share it, teach it, and embrace it without hypothesizing where it comes from, or assuming that the universe loves us when it clearly wants to turn us into worm food.

Wrapping it up

In summary, I think man inherantly needs to explain the world around him, and that his imagination makes up answers to that which he can't explain. This leads to superstition, which leads to religion, which leads to organized religion. If you take what's in place and follow it back through history to its roots, you'll find a scared little caveman huddled next to a fire, worried about all the things, imagined or real, out in the darkness waiting to eat him. For that reason, I see no reality in religion, despite how long it has been around.

Danny, instead of this book "proving to you that God does not exist" I hope that it shows you what I believe and how I came to believe it. I hope that it helps you understand how I feel about people who want to push their religion on others, through friendly persuasion or through threats. And I hope that it helps you see that if we have to have religion in our lives, it should be used for good, for comfort, caring and to make you a better person and a better member of the human race; not to give you an excuse to hate someone else because their beliefs are different from yours. I hope you can laugh at the silly traditions, symbolism and myths that have been handed down through thousands of generations and realize that in the big picture you own your religion, it doesn't own you. You should decide how your religion should make you feel and make you act, it shouldn't dictate those things for you.

For the new and existing Atheists reading this for help with the struggle you're facing in this overly-religious world, the same goes for you. You own what you believe. There is no real proof, one way or the other, when it comes to things we can't fully comprehend. If you want to take a side, then choose what you believe and stand by it. Educate yourself. If someone wants to change your mind, engage them in friendly debate or decline the invitation.

For the fundamentalists and fanatics out there who are offended by these ideas or feel hatred for people different than them, you should worry less about what other people say and believe and concentrate on what you say and believe. The same goes for the righteous hypo-crites. Didn't Jesus say, "Judge not, lest ye be judged"? That's a pretty good rule to live by.

For all the literalists who think the world is flat and that the sun re-volves around the Earth, feel free to do whatever you feel is right as long as it doesn't involve dragging the rest of us into the stone age with you.

Test Your Literalism Again

Grab that pencil! If you've read this book from front to back, and **have been diligently doodling and taking pop quizzes, here's** a re-peat of the first test presented in the introduction.

Answer Yes or No to these statements to see if you are a Biblical literalist or not. None of the answers should require any extra expla-nations or qualifications. In your opinion, these things are either true or not, without symbolism or metaphor.

Yes	No	
☐	☐	God created Adam out of dust (or clay) and then made Eve from one of Adam's ribs.
☐	☐	Jesus Christ resurrected Lazarus from the dead.
☐	☐	God flooded the Earth by causing it to rain 40 days and 40 nights, and Noah saved all the animals of the world by putting them in his boat.
☐	☐	After teaching one afternoon, Jesus fed over 5,000 people with 5 loaves of bread and 2 fish.
☐	☐	God destroyed the cities of Sodom and Gomorrah with fire and brimstone from heaven.
☐	☐	Lot's wife was turned into a pillar of salt for looking back at the destruction of Sodom as they fled the city.
☐	☐	The Rapture will occur one day, at which time Christians will vanish from the Earth and be transported to heaven.
☐	☐	Lucifer (the Devil) lives in Hell and commands legions of demons to do his bidding (like causing temptation and possessing politicians, preachers and little girls).

If you said you believe some of the things in that test but not all of them, ask yourself why. What's the difference? What makes one story from the Bible true and something else just a fairy tale? That's one of the reasons I'm an Atheist. It's obvious to me that most of those stories are just made up.

The universe is out to get us. It will win, eventually, but in the meantime, don't take life so seriously. Have a laugh.

DOODLE TIME: Draw a prophet walking his favorite camel to the watering hole.

Tips: don't forget the hot sun beating down on them, scorpions, palm trees, and the sword of justice.

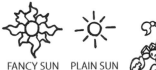

FANCY SUN   PLAIN SUN

God has chosen to appear in many forms over the years, from walking in the garden with Adam to talking to Moses as a bush. He was a disembodied voice in a cave for Mohamed and He once appeared as a toilet brush to me (just to prove a point) before I decided that He didn't exist.

BONUS DOODLE TIME: Add details of God's incarnations.

Tips: add flies to the brush, have Him say "Recite!" from the cave, and add the collateral damage from the pillar of fire, like burned-out huts and flaming Egyptian chariots.

God has evolved with civilization. When we were jealous and petty, so was God. Spiteful vendettas were common to the Old Testament Almighty. Plus, He played tricks on and tested the faith of His followers, despite the fact that He was all-knowing (and already knew if they would pass the test or not.)

DOUBLE BONUS DOODLE TIME:

Help Abraham get to the top of the mountain so he can sacrifice his son to God, as commanded.

Tips: avoid the things that will keep him from reaching God's glory.

Lazarus

Epilogue

Z arry sat on his favorite Persian blanket under a palm awning in a corner of his courtyard, sharing olives with Jeshua. The Galilean had led Zarry away from the party to the quiet place, produced two bowls of wine and called for snacks.

They spoke like old friends for hours, feelings of fraternal trust unlocked by strong wine. Zarry shared his feelings of unfulfilled potential while Jeshua described a world without Romans and authoritarian Pharisees. Each listened to the other with rapt attention while the party raged across the courtyard.

Zarry's wife had disappeared in the fray with his sisters, too busy keeping the bread and hummus platters filled and the wine flowing. She hadn't said a word to Zarry since he climbed out of the tomb because the crowd had whisked him off to his house. The party started before she and his sisters could descend upon him. Now they worked the kitchen, ordering more food and drink, and keeping the dancing girls and musicians from raising the ire of the neighbors.

"I feel like a new man," Zarry confided.

"You should," Jeshua said. He spit an olive pit onto the mountain of pits they had built between them. "You've brought a lot of hope to these hopeless people."

"Yeah." Zarry swirled the wine in his bowl and smiled at a passing dancing girl who gave him an exaggerated wink with one coal-lined eye. "It seems like a lot of people thought I was actually dead in the tomb."

Jeshua deftly swiped a new bowl of olives from a server's tray, unnoticed. "Probably best if we don't discourage them from thinking that." He placed the olives between them. Zarry grabbed one and savored its oily richness.

A juggler approached and stood before Jeshua with his pins

tucked under his armpit. He scowled at the mystic before growling, "it's been three hours."

Jeshua smiled at the man, ever pleasant, "Already? Three hours?" He offered some pita bread but the juggler shook his head.

"Hmm," Jeshua patted his hips and belt, then looked to Zarry. "Think this party is going to last another three hours?"

"I think it'll last all night," Zarry said with a smile, tapping his foot to the beat of the drummers accompanying the dancers.

"Any chance you could pay this fine man for more juggling?"

Zarry waved to get his house servant's attention. He cupped his palm and hefted it a few times in the universal symbol of "get my money bag," then jabbed a thumb toward the juggler. The servant bowed his understanding.

"Go, see that fellow there," Zarry said to the juggler, indicating his servant, "and ask him to pay for six hours."

The juggler nodded and crossed the courtyard, tossing his pins in the air as he went.

"Jugglers," Jeshua said with a shrug, "always want to be paid up front. Won't barter. Never donate their time for a good cause. Won't take the promise of eternal salvation as fair compensation. Must be something to do with their union, I guess."

They laughed and toasted the eternal order of jugglers loudly to the cheering crowd. Then the sisterhood of scarfed dancers. The royal order of drummers and brotherhood of shiskabob cooks followed. The revellers toasted Zarry and his household, then sang hosannas to Jeshua.

The two of them returned to their relative isolation sitting cross-legged on the carpet and raised their bowls again.

Zarry dragged one sleeve across his beard and said with a chuckle, "I don't think I've ever been happier, even though this party is going to cost me a month's salary." He chuckled again. "Oh, how my wife will scold me tomorrow!"

Jeshua stared at his feet and traced outlines of circles on his dusty arches with the tip of a finger. "Don't worry about her. Tomorrow she'll have a newfound respect for you. Everyone will." He squeezed Zarry's thigh and patted his knee.

"We've got to splurge every now and then," Jeshua said, solemnly. "Life's too short, Lazarus. Too short. You and I above all people should know that."

"Call me Zarry," Zarry said, blushing sheepishly. Then he added, "It's what my friends call me."

Jeshua contemplated it, then smiled and nodded to himself.

"Good nickname, Zarry," Jeshua said as he tossed an olive in the air and caught it in his mouth. "My mother called me her Little Miracle when I was a child. I didn't get it until I heard my parents arguing one night about a visitation from an angel while my father was out of town." He spit the pit onto the pile. "I'll call you Zarry when we're alone, but I'll have to call you Lazarus in public."

Zarry was crestfallen at first, then brightened for the comprimise. This was the kind of acceptance he had wished for, the give and take he yearned for from his wife. He couldn't wait to tell **her that Jeshua was going to start calling him Zarry and that he** predicted it would start a trend. But he was curious.

"Why call me Lazarus in public?"

Jeshua winked at him as if reading his mind and casually refilled the wine bowls.

"Because it will sound better in the story."

One more thought

Afterward

In the world as it is, now

L ight from the sunny, late spring day pours through the mountain-facing window of Thom's home office, washing the floors of his writing sanctuary and art studio with white light. ELO's greatest hits are playing on his laptop as he rewrites the scene where Marc terrorizes the elf children with a bedtime poem about a vengeful farmer. Or is it a knight? Since the poem is recited in first person, it's hard to tell unless he adds a line that describes the narrator. Thom shakes his head, bringing himself back from the tangent he unexpectedly embarked upon.

The doorbell rings.

Thom walks down the steps from his office, glances out the window at the young man standing on the porch and opens the door. He notices that the visitor is holding a worn copy of the book he wrote a year before.

Thom greets the stranger through the screen door, "Hi."

The stranger is tall, that hasn't-stopped-growing-yet awkward appearance of being stretched, accentuated by the sleeves of a jacket too short and high-water pants revealing black dress socks clinging to pale ankles above sneakers that have experienced a few too many basketball games. A ragged backpack hangs from one strap behind his shoulder. He has close-cropped blond hair and wears a haunted look in his eyes that could be from lack of sleep or fervent purpose. A frown of confusion crosses his face. He glances from Thom to a **page in the book.**

"Um, are you Thom Phelps?"

Thom smiles. "Yes. Can I help you?"

The stranger holds up the dog-eared book, the cover photo of two bare feet, creased and stained, facing Thom. "Did you write this?"

"Yes, I did." A warning siren goes off in Thom's head. *WEEooo! Psycho! WEEooo! Psycho!* He pushes it aside. This could be a kid who wants an autograph, he tells himself. There haven't been many of those, besides friends and family, so be gracious. Still, his grip on the doorknob tightens and he steadies himself with his other hand on the doorframe.

"Um, my name is Billy Chapman."

"Hi, Billy. Nice to meet you."

"I, uh, I'm from Salt Lake. I read your book."

A fan. Thom breathes a sigh of relief. Still, how did he know where I lived?

"I rode the bus here. It's, um, about fourteen hours. I read it again on the bus. That's like the third time."

Thom decides not to make a joke about the book not being good enough for one read, let alone three. He opts for gracious instead of facetious.

"Did you walk here from the bus station?" Thom measured the distance in his head from downtown. Maybe ten miles. "Do you want to come in and have a drink of water or something?"

Thom swings the front door open and reaches for the storm door. As his fist closes on the handle he freezes. Billy is pointing a .38 revolver at him. Tears well up in Billy's eyes. Thom can't tell if they are tears of anger or sadness.

With pistol hand shaking, Billy says, "You don't look like your picture."

He pulls the trigger twice.

The roar of the shots hurts Thom's ears more than the sensation of being punched in the chest. His legs give way and he slumps to the floor, falling back onto the carpeted stairs. There's a burning sensation on his left cheek where a shard of glass from the shattering storm door cut him. Warm blood pours down the side of face, mixing with the tears from his smarting left eye. The smell of gun powder fills his nostrils and throat, burning the roof of his mouth.

He coughs once and starts to laugh at himself. The only thing he can think of is how hard it was for he and his wife to install that storm door and what a pain it will be to have to replace it.

Deafened by the shots, Thom can't hear Billy explaining that God forgives him for insulting Jesus Christ and Joseph Smith, nor that they will pray for his soul and baptize him into the church, now that he's paid restitution for his apostasy. He's completely numb, aside from the burning cut on his cheek, shock dulling his senses and distracting his thoughts from the killer kneeling on his front porch. In fact, he's forgotten about Billy as he tries to remember the best way to get fresh blood out of carpet. Is it coarse salt or white wine?

The high-pitched ringing in his ears gives way to the sounds of calling voices and a distant firetruck's siren. In his narrowing field of vision, silhouettes of neighbors move between Thom and the blue sky beyond his porch's stoop.

In a world without religious fundamentalists

L ight from the sunny, late spring day pours through the mountain-facing window of Thom's home office, washing the floors of his writing sanctuary and art studio with white light. ELO's greatest hits are playing on his laptop as he rewrites the scene where Marc terrorizes the elf children with a bedtime poem about a vengeful farmer. Or is it a knight? Since the poem is recited in first person, it's hard to tell unless he adds a line that describes the narrator. Thom shakes his head, bringing himself back from the tangent he unexpectedly embarked upon.

The doorbell rings.

Thom walks down the steps from his office, glances out the window at the young man standing on the porch and opens the door. He notices that the visitor is holding a worn copy of the book he wrote a year before.

Thom greets the stranger through the screen door, "Hi."

The stranger is tall, that hasn't-stopped-growing-yet awkward appearance of being stretched, accentuated by the sleeves of a jacket too short and high-water pants revealing black dress socks clinging to pale ankles above sneakers that have experienced a few too many basketball games. A ragged backpack hangs from one strap behind his shoulder. He has close-cropped blond hair and wears a weary look in his eyes that could be from lack of sleep or fervent purpose. Confusion crosses his face. He glances from Thom to a page in the book.

"Um, are you Thom Phelps?"

Thom smiles. "Yes. Can I help you?"

The stranger holds up the dog-eared book, the cover photo of two bare feet, creased and stained, facing Thom. "Did tou write this?"

"Yes, I did." A warning siren goes off in Thom's head. *WEEooo! Psycho! WEEooo! Psycho!* He pushes it aside. This could be a kid who wants an autograph, he tells himself. There haven't been many of those, besides friends and family, so be gracious. Still, his grip on the doorknob tightens and he steadies himself with his other hand on the doorframe.

"Um, my name is Billy Chapman."

"Hi, Billy. Nice to meet you."

"I, uh, I'm from Salt Lake. I read your book."

A fan. Thom breathes a sigh of relief. Still, how did he know where I lived?

"I rode the bus here. It's, um, about fourteen hours. I read it again on the bus. That's like the third time."

Thom decides not to make a joke about the book not being good enough for one read, let alone three. He opts for gracious instead of facetious.

"Did you walk here from the bus station?" Thom measured the distance in his head from downtown. Maybe ten miles. "Do you want to come in and have a drink of water or something?"

Thom swings the front door aside and opens the storm door.

"Um, yeah. I mean, yes. Water would be good." Billy steps through the threshold and lumbers past Thom into the living room.

"Have a seat. Take a load off." Thom ushers Billy to the couch then crosses to the kitchen where he fills two glasses of water from the tap. "Did you like it?" Thom dreaded the answer.

"Well," Billy hesitates, "it's, um, really not written very good. Kind of, like, all over the place."

Thom smiles to himself at Billy's grammar. Then says, half-heartedly serious, "yeah, I've thought about that, but decided it was necessary, considering the primary audience."

"Danny?"

"Yeah."

"Is he real? Did he really poison that dog?"

"Yeah. He's real." Thom returns from the kitchen with the drinks and a saucer of cookies. He hands Billy a glass and places the cookies on the coffee table. Billy gulps his water, emptying half the glass, then reaches for a cookie.

"Has he read it?"

"I think so. I sent him a copy, and he called me a few weeks later to say he never preached to me or tried to convert me."

"Are you still friends?"

"Of course. We talk all the time. He even sent me some doodles from the book that he drew. But, let's talk about why you're here. A bus ride from Salt Lake City is a long way."

"Yeah." Billy takes another gulp of water. "I, uh, was wondering about the doodles." He reaches into his backpack and pulls out a stack of paper. He smooths them on the coffee table and starts handing them to Thom, one at a time. "I Googled you and found out where you live. I hope that's okay."

Thom rolls his eyes, "The Internet is a wonderful thing." He examines the first sheet of sketch paper. It depicts a monstrously evil-looking BoGo the Devourer wreaking havoc on downtown Tokyo. Thom chuckles. The next page is a full color pen and ink illustration, a-la Frank Miller, of God as a pillar of fire, carving the Ten Commandments into two slabs of rock.

"Wow. You're really good. You should draw comic books or get a job as an illustrator some day."

"Thanks. I didn't want to e-mail these or just upload them to your web site. I was, uh, wondering if you you'd like to buy some of them? In fact I am writing a comic book with a friend, and we're going to try to sell it to a publisher."

Thom smiled. That's a long bus ride to sell some drawings to a stranger, he thought. He probably won't make back his outlay for bus fare. I'll offer him thirty bucks for each.

"Sure. I'd like to have some of these. What's your price?"

"Um, look. I want to get something out in the open. I know you're an Atheist and all..." Billy trails off and focuses on another cookie.

"Shoot."

"I, uh, believe in God. And that Jesus is my personal savior."

"Okay. And?"

"And you'd still want to buy these drawings?"

Thom chuckles. "Definitely. Let's take a look and see how many will work for me. After all, you bought my book, right?"

Billy smiles and presses into the chair, relaxing a bit.

"Ya know," Thom says as he shuffles through the drawings, separating them into stacks, "you kind of worried me, coming to my house uninvited. You could have just sent me an e-mail saying you wanted to sell me these. Spammers do it all the time. Everything from vitamins to adult web sites."

"Yeah, but you probably would've turned me down."

Thom shrugs and nods. "True. I probably would have." He straightens the stack of his favorites. "I'll take these six."

Billy sits up. "Great. How's a hundred bucks each?"

The Gay Jesus Cartoon

Let's talk more about my cartoon of a gay
Jesus. Is it funny? It makes me chuckle, but
would it make others laugh? Maybe, maybe
not. (Most people, probably not.)

That's the problem with humor, it's totally subjective.
To each his own. What is funny to one person might be offensive to
another.

In our culture, we laugh at a lot of things, serious and not-so-serious.
It's how we deal with tough subjects, how we lighten the mood, and,
sure, how we get a rise out of someone. As Steve Martin once noted
with the title of an album, "Comedy is not pretty." We make jokes
about all manner of subjects that are taboo to different segments of
society, from the Holocaust and pedophilia to animal abuse, racism,
and spousal abuse. The question is whether or not the joke is delivered with malice.

I didn't draw this cartoon with malicious intent. Yes, I admit I wholeheartedly meant for it to push some people's comfort zone buttons,
but only as an absurdity and not as an insult. It's absurd to think that
as He was dying on the cross Jesus lamented that He never got to
"wrestle" with the object of His homoerotic affection, a-la *The Last
Temptation of Christ*. The joke just as easily could have been about
him dreading the trip he was about to take ("Did I forget to turn off
the oven?") or poke fun at the Mormons ("Oh, great. Now I have
to make an appearance in the New World to a bunch of corn-eating
savages. I should fire my agent.") That's funny, but might also of-
fend some people in the LDS church.

The cartoon would have been malicious, though, if I had cruelly
depicted Jesus performing some deviant act that implies I hate Him.
How far can you go before you cross the line? In humor, there's a
huge gray area, and that's hard for people to accept when they only
think in black-and-white.

About the author

Thom Phelps is a screenwriter and graphic artist. He lives in a clothing-optional commune in the shadow of Focus on the Family's headquarters.

In his spare time he skis, grows herbs, and takes orders from his neighbor's talking dog.

Visit www.ToenailsBook.com for Doodle Time refills.

1713147